THE AESTHETICS OF THE JAPANESE LUNCHBOX

Kenji Ekuan

edited by David B. Stewart

The MIT Press

Cambridge, Massachusetts   London, England

Translated by Don Kenny.

This book was set in Garamond 3 and Stone Sans
Printed and bound in Italy by Milanostampa

Library of Congress Cataloging-in-Publication Data

Ekuan, Kenji, 1929–
      [Makunouchi bentō no bigaku. English]
      The aesthetics of the Japanese lunchbox / Kenji Ekuan : edited by David B. Stewart.
        p. cm.
      Includes bibliographical references and index.
      ISBN 0-262-05055-2 (hc : alk. paper)
      1. Japan—Civilization. 2. Aesthetics, Japanese. I. Stewart, David B. II. Title.
      DS821.E49513 1998
      952—dc21   97- 40056
                                                                                      CIP

Dedicated to Arthur J. Pulos

Arthur was a very big-hearted man. He was also deeply interested in Japanese culture. Through our joint work for ICSID, we traveled all over Asia, including Japan.

I was greatly stimulated by the theories of American design that he expressed in his books *American Design Ethic* and *The American Design Adventure,* as were most designers, particularly those of my generation. When I told him I had written this book to demonstrate that there is a Japanese theory of design culture, Arthur expressed interest, and it was through his influence that MIT decided to publish it.

Arthur always insisted upon design as civilization, strongly stressing the role played by design in the history of culture. So, appropriately enough, it is through our mutual understanding and aspirations in the midst of our design activities that this new English-language version of my book has come into being.

In 1995, Arthur died, but I am certain that when he sees this book from the beyond, he will praise it, saying, "Well done." And that he will then give me a new stack of homework to carry my ideas further. For I feel sure that as long as this book exists, Arthur will be keeping an eye on me, as if to say, "Kenji, there is a dream for the human race in design."

Kenji Ekuan

CONTENTS

Dazzling Nothingness—A Pretext

I remember once spending an entire day entertaining a guest from abroad. We became so engrossed in talking about the world and Japan that we forgot the passage of time, until suddenly we saw the setting sun and our hearts were stolen by the spectacle of the evening sky. For an instant, the fiercely burning sun turned to a clearly outlined, perfect disk. Then it dropped quickly behind the mountaintops and disappeared.

After that concentrated instant as a circle of light, the sun had precipitately dropped out of sight; *nothingness* began. I found myself sitting in speechless admiration before the ever-changing phenomena of nature. Then I was overcome by a sort of sadness and confusion—wondering who, or what, those of us involved in designing *artificial* forms might call our teacher.

Coming back to myself with a start, I realized it was time to invite my guest to the table where a meal had been prepared. That day it was a make-do sort of cold meal easy to order from a nearby restaurant on the spur of the moment, yet comprising the best possible ingredients—the *makunouchi bento* or Japanese lunchbox. Fearing that the little sectionalized wooden container might seem too plain and simple to my guest, I placed a single blossom on its lid as a decoration.

As the guest took his seat his eye darted to the blossom on the lid. The lacquer of the box provided a gently luminous background that brought the flower to pulsating life, and we experienced a moment of almost prayerlike silence. I broke this with an explanation of the daily arts of flower arrangement and tea ceremony that young women still often learn as part of good housekeeping.

I pointed out that arrangement or placement of a single blossom is the acme of the art—the ultimate aim of this etiquette of ritualized aesthetic creation being to invoke the beauty of *all* flowers, of beauty itself, of all dazzling elegance by a single instance—to reduce the many to the one. Suddenly we experienced again the brilliant split second of clarity when the sun had become a perfect disk. I picked up the blossom and put it on the table; then I lifted the lid off my lunchbox. And my guest followed suit.

He exclaimed in surprise at the universe of color and variety hidden inside the diminutive square lacquered box. He deliberately replaced the lid, setting the flower back on top of it. Then he again removed first the flower and then the lid. He was savoring once more that first shock of surprise. And during this repetition he exclaimed, *"Beautiful!"*

He told me that he could clearly sense the reduction of the *many* to the *one* that I had expounded as the core concept of the lunchbox.

He found that the contrast of the vastly varied colors of the evening sky with the clear, bright disk of the sun rebounded in the contrast between the single blossom and the lunchbox. I explained that this is how we in Japan discover masters, or our teachers. The lunchbox has been refined and perfected over several hundred years. If we were to analyze to the profoundest limit the history of this lunchbox—the spirit of its form and aesthetics—we might discover the secret essence of that technology which has made it possible for Japan to survive in the world. I felt the greatest urge to point out the ways in which we have succeeded in using and compounding to the full all the valuable technology of form that underlies the daily life of the Japanese.

The single blossom arrangement and the lunchbox. I found myself wanting to draw all possible conclusions from the simple severity of these forms and to explain them in so systematic and simple a manner that anyone might understand. The result of my efforts is the present book, in which I discuss "things Japanese" in the context of both their form and our traditional lifestyle.

In the introduction that follows, I begin with a repertory of basic ways to enjoy the lunchbox. I shall then detail the process of discovery of the spirit of form in general, as found among the people of Japan.

In Part One, "Hidden Aspects of the Lunchbox," I enumerate and describe some forty-eight attitudes (or modes) comprised in the Japanese etiquette of form as embodied in the lunchbox. I attempt thus to reveal fully the source of the Japanese style of making things. Then I shall demonstrate how these techniques for the creation of lunchbox-type things are still frequently employed, in various guises, in the daily life of Japan today.

In Part Two, "Lunchbox-Style Interpretation of Japanese Industry," I take a look at the ways in which the etiquette of formal determination I explained in Part One is embodied in such contemporary Japanese products as mini-calculators, cars, and package tours, as well as how such traditional items as Buddhist altars and tea houses reappear in altered forms in contemporary life. Thus, throughout this book, I shall propose a certain way of looking at things Japanese. Meanwhile, I believe that this way of looking can lead to solutions to most of our design problems.

To sum up, the introduction explains the development process of the variety of ideals generated by the lunchbox. Part One presents my theories regarding the creative power of the structure of the lunchbox. And Part Two is a compilation of related aspects of contemporary Japanese life and industry.

The final section, "Spirit of the Lunchbox—Globalization of Japan," outlines my conclusions and predictions for the future. The spirit of form exemplified in the Japanese lunchbox points to an ingenious technology that will help preserve a rich legacy for the future. In what follows I have explained how I believe this technology should be exploited and how its merits may be conveyed to the rest of the world.

Finally, I have added "A Brief History of the Lunchbox" to provide background information on the lunchbox itself—its unique physical structure and development, classical forms and variations.

The book was written to express theories of form and design that have evolved from my admiration for the beauty of the lunchbox; techniques of organization and production born of an appreciation of its structure; a notion of the tradition that has always been at the root of the Japanese "way of making things" as revealed in contemporary industry; and a glimpse of the future as predicted from the basic principles of Japanese lifestyle exhibited in the makeup of the lunchbox.

Pausing to think about all this, I realize that I have put in so many different things that the book itself may have become a true product of the lunchbox mentality. Perhaps my efforts accurately expose the nature of the lunchbox-oriented Japanese mind.

The inspiration for writing came originally from a visit I received by an editor on behalf of the Goma Publishing Company in Tokyo. He arrived at my door bearing a clipping from the *Mainichi News* of an article I had written to hint at some of the possibilities of an eventual lunchbox theory. The editor suggested developing the theory in full-length book form from that tiny news item that lay in the palm of his hand. I was amazed at his wit and determination, and I wish to thank him for providing the impetus for the present volume, now reissued in English to reach a still wider public.

THE AESTHETICS OF THE JAPANESE LUNCHBOX

A Look at the Blossom Archipelago

The greatest pleasure of the lunchbox comes when you take off the lid and sit for a moment gazing at the various delights inside. No matter how many times I open a lunchbox, I find myself gulping in surprise at its gorgeous contents.

It inevitably contains delicacies from the sea, from the mountains, and from the plains in a variety of colors and fragrances. But you never have the feeling of unsightly clutter or congestion. The array of tidbits is divided into separate compartments with a sense of order, and without ever mixing together. There is a marvelous discipline here—a power of form that amply allows for plurality. Where does it derive from?

Whenever I look down into a lunchbox, I feel an image of the Japanese archipelago rise to the surface. Japan has the lovely traditional name of the Flower Chain Islands. Peering into the lunchbox, you might almost be staring down from high in the air at these islands with all their variation packed into narrow confines.

We Japanese boast a long history of residing in the narrow space of our land; this appears to have resulted in the deep engraving of a compact way of life in our very genes and to have nurtured a corresponding aesthetic sense. I cannot help but consider the lunchbox as virtually an emblem of the land itself.

The lifestyle and practices that have made it possible for us Japanese to create a good life for ourselves within a rather unfavorable environment, made up of many mountains with only a few fertile plains, poor natural resources, and a high population density, has metamorphosed, so to speak, into a technology for giving birth to unusual forms of beauty. But the impetus behind the creation of the amazing sense of order found in the lunchbox must be something more than this. I would hazard that the power of form revealed here is supported by something like a persisting passion to convert poverty into wealth.

It is poor manners to start eating the instant you remove the lid of the lunchbox. You must allow your eyes time to peruse and enjoy the food before moving on to gratify the

2

1

A square, black-lacquered lunchbox is presented to a guest with a single blossom placed on top, yielding a sense of expectation and tension similar to that experienced in the theater just before the opening of the curtain. (Photo by Takeshi Doi, with cooperation of Japanese restaurant Ichie)

2

Shokado-style *makunouchi* lunchbox. One of the pleasures of the lunchbox is to gaze at the contents for a time after taking off the lid. It is full of delicacies from both mountain and sea, but the viewer never receives a sense of confusion. The arrangement is dominated by an esoteric order—a state of tension that creates a delicately variegated beauty. (Photo by Takeshi Doi, with cooperation of Japanese restaurant Ichie)

taste buds. There are thus two levels of enjoyment, and herein lies the wealth of the lunch-box. Compared to the direct pursuit of pleasure that is nearly universal nowadays, this seems a most extraordinary wealth indeed. Has not our placidly persistent avarice engendered a form that, with regard to the lunchbox, demands that we stop to measure the visual component in full before taking chopsticks in hand to savor the actual taste? Is it not this *greed*, impelling enjoyment of a single object on multiple levels, that has made the products of Japan—born in the context of such limited natural and spatial resources—so extraordinarily beautiful?

The Creator's Disposition

The habit of enjoying things first with the eyes is an integral part of the Japanese lifestyle. And it is something that foreign visitors will inadvertently imitate, even for the first time, on seeing a Japanese gaze at his or her food before lifting the chopsticks. Once more, what is the source of this disposition toward creating scenery even in a lunchbox? Is not such an attitude proof positive that there exists a more profound greed in the creator than in the consumer? It would appear that the creator is instinctively disposed to concoct a beauty so compelling that the partaker, as if bound by nature, will stop to gaze at the food in front of him before grasping the chopsticks to eat.

A Unified-World Mandala

Things from the sea and things from the mountains; boiled, fried, and sautéed items; sweet, spicy, and sour condiments; red, white, and green shapes—a veritable landscape would seem inadequate to accord order to such numerous and disparate elements. But we find them all harmoniously arranged in the mere foot-square space of a lunchbox. Would it not require true genius to accomplish the same feat with either people or objects?

But lunchbox "artists" would most likely reply that no sort of genius is involved at all, rather it is merely a matter of setting things together in the most commonplace and logical manner—something that anyone might be able to do, with at most a minimum of training and practice. It is a technique that everyone holds in common: thus, the enjoyment of the lunchbox lies in savoring this instinct of the creator, who has simply acted on impulse for the sake of the joy and appreciation of the partaker. And the person able to enjoy the act of consuming the lunch becomes an automatic gourmet genius. The etiquette and structure of the lunchbox make geniuses of both creator and eater. In other words, the lunchbox itself supplies this genius.

The Eye Enjoys Order

The creation of form is discovery of order, a unification of disparate objects. But it must also be conceded that the lunchbox possesses an implicit and strict hierarchy. Without such, it would hardly be capable of greater consequence. A highly sophisticated system is essential to contain and display to full effect such varied individual components. The refined ideology of a ruler or monarch imbues the graceful form of boiled or marinated foods when placed inside the lunchbox.

A Makeshift Art

The average lunchbox is a makeshift device, a resource in emergency situations, a temporary stopgap measure. This requisite application in accordance with circumstance is an "invisible system" pervading all levels of form-creation sensitivity in Japan. This brisk meeting of conditions such as deadline, place, difficulty of obtaining materials, cost adjustment, and timing—all contingent in terms of time, quality, and quantity—might justly be termed an Applied Technology of Circumstance. The lunchbox (or *makunouchi bento,* literally "intermission lunch") was originally a meal to be consumed at the theater. Thus it was born out of just such a technology.

The mission of the lunchbox is not only to coincide with a particular time frame, but also to fulfill certain prerequisites of content as well. When you remove the lid and observe the contents beneath, you will invariably discover something you can enjoy eating no matter what your food likes and dislikes. You might not be completely satisfied, but at least you will be rescued from starvation. The inclusion of so many different items presumes a certain economy of waste, but advantage lies in the fact that the largest possible variety of tastes will be placated. Stopping to review our discussion, one cannot help but feel that the fundamental principles behind the creation of the lunchbox meal that we Japanese partake of almost daily with barely a second thought are pregnant with an extremely modern wisdom.

The Concept of Universal Salvation

As the lunchbox structure is by intention all things to all people, salvation is a foregone conclusion. Our lunchbox is scarcely for the ostentatious display of high-quality or unusual delicacies but instead gathers together normal, familiar, everyday things from nature, according to season, and enhances their inherent appeal. It even includes unnecessary items. If you objectively analyze these ingredients all lined up together, you will quickly discern which are superior and which inferior. But once arranged within the structure of the lunchbox, even the commonplace assumes a vibrant life. Here we discover the greatness of the submission of all things to the context of the Japanese worldview. The aim of preparation and arrangement revealed in the lunchbox is to include everything and bring each to full life. Herein lies the essence of the Japanese stance of all-inclusive assimilation and the concept of "universal salvation." Through an inclusion of all foods, all people—whatever their likes or dislikes—are provided with a safety net.

The lunchbox meal is largely mass-produced. Thus problems of cost must be addressed. It was surely for this reason that the technique of bringing commonplace foodstuffs to life was first introduced. This lends a certain logic to the waste inherent in maintaining a broad appeal, helping us to see that the lunchbox system has with relative ease overcome one of the most difficult issues faced by today's imperative of mass production. The lunchbox embodies a truly marvelous production theory.

A vessel sets the limits of the world of the lunchbox—namely, a flat box, a surface surrounded by a shallow frame, a microcosm emblematic of a vast landscape in one square foot. If too large, it would immediately lose its aura of compactness. If too small, it would revert to an entirely different structure. It appears that there is a unique thesis of space-and-frame in this just-right size of the lunchbox.

A Many-Talented National Character

The aesthetic of greed that introduces disparate elements while heightening the individual characteristics of each has given birth to an economy of structure that depends on strict selection of the size of the container or vessel. The background against which such wisdom has been cultivated lies in the history of Japan, as typified by recurrent introduction and utilization to the full, deepening and harvesting the best from quite disparate cultures and civilizations. The physical area of Japan itself is a "vessel" limited by sea surrounding it on all sides. And it may now be claimed with confidence that, since Japan has at long last established itself as an industrial nation, we have demonstrated our multi-talented national character to the world at large.

The etiquette of formal creation revealed in the structure of the lunchbox remains part of our inheritance. The newer products of Japan, so packed full of enjoyment, fascinate the rest of the world. The mini-calculator is full of "delicacies" rendering possible multiplicity of operations at the touch of a button. The compact Japanese automobile is fitted with everything from power steering to air conditioner, stereo tape-deck, computerized direction finder, and cellular phone, with the most remarkable tenacity of purpose.

Thoughts on the Maturation of Industry

Today the key theme for the realization of our desires is visual function measurable in terms of physical performance. Industry has worked to create products that are faster, stronger, bigger, and more efficient. But we Japanese are presently in the process of pursuing a different direction, training the sights of our greed toward both higher quality and ever more human texture.

Examining the phenomenon of industrial maturity, we find a great lesson to be learned from the fact that the lunchbox meal, in which it was necessary to marshal a large number of foods and preparation skills, has nevertheless always given priority to beauty. If we work in the direction suggested by this tradition, it is most probable that a new and unexpected type of beauty will emerge in the midst of industrial society.

The joys of the lunchbox are limitless in terms of the various levels of arrangement and juxtaposition it affords. Thinking along such lines, one's imagination takes flight, each new thought leading to another in a vision of sustained creativity. As we soar in our flights of fancy, we find this position affords a good bird's-eye view of Japan's natural and human resources and skills.

The lunchbox structure sprang from and intensified a spirit of creativity able to transcend the physical poverty of our land. It made use of techniques of observation and cultivated a sensitivity to the mutual relatedness of all things. Today there is need to work to further promote lunchbox structure in various areas of our present complex and troubled society. It would be contemptible to waste this capacity for form that appears to flow in our very veins.

Ten Axioms of Lunchbox Structure

- Beauty of Form—drive to make stylishness and beauty a primary function.
- Functional Multiplicity—belief in "the more functions the better."
- Equipment Exciting Creativity—popular appeal yielding the broadest possible application of an object and its creative uses.
- Prototype—an exacting model promoting sound fabrication and generating ideas for use.
- Unification in Diversity—a sense of order ensuring maximal inclusion and effective arrangement.
- All-Inclusive Enhancement—plurality in each element vividly brought to life.
- Profusion of Enjoyment—development capacity from which new types of enjoyment emerge.
- Ultimate Adaptability—meeting needs in terms of time, quality, and quantity.
- Waste-Avoiding Culture—a sense of design consistent with environmentally sensitive lifestyle.
- Generosity—richness born from an ultimate spirit of service.

These ten principles of the lunchbox aesthetic and its etiquette of production and use will be expounded chapter by chapter in Part One.

3
The Japanese archipelago is sometimes referred to by the lovely traditional name of the Flower-Chain Islands, owing to the varied natural beauty within the confines of its narrow land form. (Photo: NNP Library)

Hidden Aspects of the Lunchbox—Japanese Etiquette of the Creation of Forms

The major asset of the lunchbox is its beauty. There is always a reason, or motivation, and a set of conditions for giving birth to anything. Among the various products we see emerging today, it appears to me that there are very few for which the motivation and conditions of production are a stated—or implicit—desire to see something beautiful.

Such qualities as ease of use, convenience, no frills, and logicality, when applied to food, tend to bear upon the realm of nutritional value. The world of flavor and beauty, however, lies beyond that level. It is hardly as if there were no nutritional value in the lunchbox meal. There is an excellent nutritional balance of foods from sea, mountains, and plains—affording a balance of flavors as well as health value. After a commodity brilliantly fulfills its functions, which is of course a necessity, what more could one hope for than to discover pleasure in the realm of beauty? It is easy enough to account for nutritional value, ease of use, convenience, and no extras. But beauty cannot be so simply explained. As we review the aims of modern functional rationalism, we cannot forever remain at the level of necessity. Much that surpasses this level, beautiful and wonderful things, came into being in the context of classical technology. Unless we first establish the logical and functional identity of a thing as a matter of course and then strive toward beauty as a function of need, we will never approach our goal.

Gods Dwelling in Each and Every Dish

A diversity of cultures coexist in Japan. And that is the reason the lunchbox structure is viable here. Along with the various other foods, there is always a molded shape of rice in a lunchbox meal. When boiled round-grain rice is squeezed into a compact form, it is easy to eat during a theater intermission. Up to this point, we are still in the domain of functional rationalism. In the early days, the cooked rice was squeezed into a shape that resembled a rice bale. Here we discover a self-symbolizing function. But it was only when development proceeded further that the result became a living form or shape. Small mounds of rice were originally made into the shape of bales, but later they were given such seasonal shapes as cranes, plovers, or maple leaves. Rice cooked together with ginkgo nuts is squeezed into the fanlike shape of ginkgo leaves. But whatever its shape, this portion of the rice is always meant to represent something culturally or seasonally relevant.

It is through such animist means that both the partaker and the myriad omnipresent Shinto deities *(kami)* take on life, as may be hinted at by the shapes in question.

Abstraction of the Chinese Character for Rice Paddy

The *shokado* lunchbox, or lunchbox version of the "blue plate special," is a particularly skillful variation of the makunouchi (intermission) lunchbox structure. It rejects such box shapes as the half moon or the plum blossom, remaining a forthright square box. As a result, it permits great freedom as well as simplicity of choice.

The square *shokado* lunchbox is subdivided into four smaller squares of equal size to approximate the Chinese character for "rice paddy." It is modeled after the actual shape of the paddy field where rice—the staple food of the Japanese and the major nutritional element of our civilization—is cultivated. It thus suggests four rice paddies divided by earthen ridges within which the agricultural drama of the four seasons is played out. Here we sense a spatial image pregnant with the flow of the year. And in one of the four paddies of the lunchbox, the fruit of rice cultivation is squeezed into an array of bale-shaped cylinders. In Japan, as frequently elsewhere, there is a culture of the mountains and a culture of the sea. A major recurring element of Japanese culture is the ritual of rice planting, and we are reminded by extension of other cultural themes freed to flow around the central rice-planting image by the pivotal symbolic character denoting "rice paddy."

Seeing and Thinking

We Japanese tend to think more with our eyes than our heads—a vision that is remarkably unified. Moreover, visually oriented people consider objects of beauty to partake as well of both truth and virtue. Such persons go beyond mere reason to grasp the entirety of whatever they come into contact with. Apprehending something beautiful in itself constitutes perception of the whole for this type of individual. A rapid understanding of the whole is of far greater importance than attention to small discrepancies.

During the postwar period of high economic growth in Japan, owners of small and medium-sized enterprises traveled to the West one after another. They were unable to speak the languages of the countries they visited and they paid no attention to the explanations of interpreters. They simply stared at the machines they were hoping to introduce into their businesses. This was quite enough for them to be able to perceive the inner workings. Were they to have attempted to understand the logic behind these machines, it would have wanted a great bustle of taking the machinery apart and reassembling it again. Since they were able to get a complete grasp by simply staring, they could instead make their decisions very quickly.

The same approach served us well in the era of assimilating "civilization and enlightenment" during the Meiji period (1868–1911), for example, in the building of steam locomotives. The craftspeople who built the boiler would visually appraise a new model until they completely understood it. It was thanks to this powerful ability to see *through* a thing with their eyes that we Japanese were able to catch up with Western civilization in a remarkably short time. This was, indeed, the *makunouchi* lunchbox human being with his ability to grasp diverse elements as a whole.

The rice-paddy-character-shaped *shokado* lunchbox contains, on average, five to six types of food in each of its four squares, bringing the total of colors and flavors to between twenty and twenty-five.

Anyone whose attention is not immediately attracted by what they find inside when they remove the lid of the lunchbox is not a visual person. The eyes move from one morsel of food to another. You look here and there. You gaze at one item concentratedly. You take in what it is and rearrange its relative position within your personal image of the whole. This is how the symbols are interpreted. It is through this sort of understanding that you see, and also create a yardstick for estimating the flavors you are about to savor.

Dialogue between Eye and Eye

I have discussed how we can see Japan in the *makunouchi* lunchbox. When you look at the pure white rice, you think of the autumn harvest season throughout the country; when you

5

Sliding paper partitions at Katsura Detached Palace in Kyoto. Paulownia leaves are portrayed at random, creating a free and whimsical beauty within a geometric framework. (Photo by Norio Asai, courtesy of Tankosha Publishing Co., Ltd.)

5

Bearer of beauty, a young girl presents a basket of delicacies for guests at a Doll Festival (Hina Matsuri) party. She exemplifies a culture in which beautiful things and beautiful manners together create a comprehensive aesthetic. (Photo from *Seikatsu Goyomi 1: Spring*, courtesy of Kodansha Ltd.)

see fresh slices of raw fish, or *sashimi,* you feel reassured that the coasts of Japan are immaculate; when you perceive chestnuts peeking out here and there from among one or two brilliantly colored autumn leaves you wonder how our mountain people are faring. All nature is displayed in this one-foot-square box. It is a means of expressing a worldview that corresponds to the *mandala.* A number of deities with well-ascribed roles are beautifully lined up in this one-foot-square space where they first give pleasure to the eyes, after which you slowly enjoy the feast!

Laying out this *mandala* feast with the deities of the sea, the mountains, and the plains all in their proper places makes the lunchbox meal taste as it should. This is the work of the chef, who must also have a sense of rapport with the guests who are about to partake of it. Since Japanese cooks normally prepare lunchbox meals for takeout, they have long been trained in symbolic analogies that all diners can comprehend and appreciate. The remaining problem, then, is the uncertain eyes of the guest who will consume the lunchbox meal. For beauty only deteriorates if unappreciated.

The cook is the maestro of the world of the *makunouchi* lunchbox. I mentioned earlier that since this person would naturally be disappointed if the result of such effort were eaten without a glance or a second thought, he or she works to make lunchbox meals so attractive that guests are actually reluctant to take up their chopsticks and begin eating. But even so, it is only a matter of time before the masterwork is consumed. The guest senses the formal layout even as he proceeds to break up the perfected layout. This is the inherent and paradoxical relationship between the provision and the acceptance of beauty.

Bearer of Beauty

The scenery inside a lunchbox is packed full of information—everything taken in by the eyes in an instant. And without a pause this information obtained through the eyes explodes like so many sympathetic fireworks and fuses within an inner world. Unless the various yardsticks of perception and intuition are accounted for in the psychological make-up of such beauty, its spirit continues to wander through the world. However, a complex psychology engenders its own character and a certain delicacy. The cultural question is whether or not we can retain the strength to pass on these techniques for living beautifully with whatever simple materials are at hand. For human nature would be threatened were we so single-minded that we had no place to welcome the myriad deities, enshrining them within our hearts.

Spiritual Precision

Beauty may be endowed with a somewhat violent procreational effect. It is dictatorial in its refusal of ugliness, and possesses considerable power of destruction. Used resourcefully, it becomes a purging force, for beauty is born of spiritual precision. The precision of the lunchbox is a manifestation of this, for all spiritual precision reveals itself in a precision of concrete things. Within the lunchbox, several dozen parts—each lovely in itself—are arranged in a beautiful manner. The relationship of these parts consists in a delicate, nearly invisible sensitivity that encompasses a "living" installation. This precision in terms of organization is the same quality employed to the full in our creation of industrial products. The more internalized that simple etiquette of assembly for making a lunchbox meal, the more attractive such products become. It will be understood how, by taking the lunchbox as an example of combinatory skills, we refer to a dynamic relationship. Its dynamics serve to arrange things better than a mere passive balance.

There are two general sources of this tension. One is the dynamic constituted by the valences of the various parts—a tension born from color, fragrance, place of origin, history, and handling. The other is the level of perfection of each individual part. Even in the creation of a small lacquered tea caddy, creation begins with the work of the craftsman who prepares the wood endowing its basic form; followed by that of the carver; then the skill of the craftsman who applies and reapplies the lacquer, and of the artist who paints its decorative patterns; and finally it is perfected by the efforts of the polisher. Degree of perfection in the industrial arts is thus proportional to an attentive division of labor among these various craftspersons. But this presumes faultless perfection at every stage. If the material is imperfect, the carving cannot be achieved; if the carving is not faultless, the lacquering and painting cannot be carried out; and if the lacquering and painting are not flawless, no luster will appear no matter how much the tea caddy is polished.

6

Tea caddy decorated with a willow tree pattern. Small enough to hold in the palm of the hand, it is the crystallization of the skills of a range of craftsmen created through a long, detailed process involving carver, lacquerer, and painter. All these work in unison to produce the artistic tension found in this tiny functional artifact. (Photo: Nezu Museum of Arts and Crafts, Tokyo)

This is the extent to which striving for perfection must be carried. And herein lies a tense mutual relation of dependence among all the different craftsmen involved. These forms once brought to bear on the production of, say, a tea caddy are once more to the fore nowadays in such Japanese products as mini-calculators and in our cozily compact cars.

Character Artistically Arranged

The lunchbox contains many different ingredients. As we have seen, there are multiple levels of beauty in the production of a single lacquered tea caddy. And the same may be said of the calculator and the automobile—not to mention more complex electronic products. Delicacy, as well as tension, is necessary to achieve skillful arrangement of elements. Thought is required to rescue the bad and bring out the best in weak things, or to hide the unsightly. Beauty brought to accomplishment through gathering many different qualities and elements reveals itself in a "nonviolent" loveliness, radiating tolerance and acceptance.

2 Flexible Functionality

An Acquisitive Nature

The Japanese are by nature acquisitive people. We cultivate more types of agricultural products and have a larger variety of foods than any other nation. In the field of sports as well, we have introduced games from all over the world, which, added to traditional indigenous pastimes and the martial arts, combine to give Japan the greatest variety of sports anywhere. The same thing can be said of music. We never seem to abandon the old and are constantly introducing the new. Along with our own myriad deities, we welcome those of all other religions and entertain and provide for them. There are any number of examples of gods and goddesses who, having lost favor in their places of origin, come to Japan where they are overjoyed at the excitement they stimulate and the gorgeous hospitality received here. But to return to our discussion of the lunchbox, what is the reason behind its birth and skillful cultivation? While there are a large number of concerns at work, the fact of the matter is that we Japanese have had little alternative but to learn to approach all things in the spirit of the lunchbox.

The Function of All-Inclusive Assimilation

The *mandala*—which originated in India as a guide to ideal spiritual frontiers—consists of the Dainichi Buddha in the center, symbol of Wisdom and source of all other beings. He is surrounded by numerous subsidiary deities regulating all manner of mundane passions and desires, with the deities of other lesser religions placed in the outermost circle. The iconographical genius of the mandala lies in the fact that at a glance you can ascertain your own position—not least your level of emancipation from worldly attachments—within the scheme of worldly passions depicted.

Human greed is *karma*, and the cessation of all desire is nirvana, or paradise. In the mundane sphere, desire is satiated by the functional aspect of things. The notion of inclusive assimilation likewise attempts to appease all desires; when applied to pleasure, it is

7

The visitor to a traditional Japanese garden enjoys changing scenery while strolling in the landscape, with a fresh view revealed at each turn of the path. This stroll garden affords detailed pleasure within a spatiotemporal continuum. (Photo: NNP Library)

similar to a health spa, where a little of each sort of pleasure is provided on an equal footing. You can experience these joys in the order you prefer. It is thus similar to the lunchbox structure, but lacks the quality of beauty. There are places that you may wish to visit once but not over and over, as well as places to which you may want to return any number of times. The quality of the welcome determines the difference. Similarly, there are many businesses that fall into a slump owing to officiousness, negligence, or an overly patronizing tone toward the public. As soon as an enterprise becomes unsuccessful, there is a tendency to turn to vulgar advertising appeals—but such is the road to hell. By contrast, when the essence of desire is addressed, the result is like a beautiful lunchbox: a view of paradise is born. But why is it that in Japan we all seem to want everything at once?

It is because we have an intuition of the true "essence" of everything here. Even to the tiniest insect belongs a complex five-part soul; each tree and blade of grass is a deity. It is owing to this grasp of the value of each entity that nothing is abandoned. It is because we Japanese perceive the essence of things that we value each one. We cannot bring ourselves to relinquish a single one of them. Greed metamorphoses as obsession, and this leads on to foolish action. Among the folktales of old Japan, there are many that warn against greed. Greedy old men and women have long been tormented as horrible examples by moralists. It is only natural that people become increasingly greedy as they grow older, since they believe themselves to have grasped the true nature of things in the course of their lives. The theory of greed illustrated in these old tales speaks implicitly to a division into greed for beauty as well as for ugliness.

No Vindication for Greed

Whatever is unable to approach the vibrant essence of greed becomes seedy and impoverished because its greed is too shallow. Instances of trifling self-justification are nothing more than insufficient greed. Offering functional explanations is little more than an attempt at vindication for producing something not worth the trouble in the first place.

To take a different example, if we really desire an attractive city, some sort of budget for clean-up and renewal will materialize. But just because of that, it does not follow that the city will be well and truly beautified. We may indeed hope to produce a fine cityscape for our descendants, but the budget issue remains, so the question then turns on the precise amount needed to create the "city beautiful." Beauty is the sum total of desire as well as its bottom line. The lunchbox goes beyond tawdry excuses. Since it is truly greedy, it has come out impeccably arranged. When greed is shallow, everything remains in confusion. It is due to the very fact that the lunchbox contains such a variety of foods that finally they are all brought equally to life with none attempting to dominate another and with none receiving unfair treatment, resulting in an enhanced and intensified coexistence. The contents are so well balanced as to satisfy the taste of *any* guest. This imparts the confidence of a universal principle of selectivity each time a lunchbox meal is served. Such requirements as obtaining ingredients, cost, the number of guests to be served, and timing can be easily met. Lunchboxes are clean, light, and easy to transport. They are a joy for the chef, and those who eat them evince surprise at the panache with which the meal has been put together. Thus, as has been said, the lunchbox affords enjoyment and satisfaction for everyone owing to the splendidly favorable impression it produces.

By analogy, I imagine how wonderful it would be if this type of city could be created. Instead of wracking one's brain over such details as an attractive business district, a luxuriant cityscape, and so on, if the decision were taken to include from the start everything that makes up the list of advantages—as in the lunchbox—everything would soon fall into its rightful place. The lunchbox spirit is such as to call forth a joy in one's surroundings—whether in the home, a bright and well-laid-out central square, or some more localized communal setting—all on account of a clear-cut and inclusive notion of order.

Enjoyment of Change

The lunchbox makes full use of the basic principle I mentioned earlier of unchangingness even though its physical size may vary with circumstance. Necessary elements are carefully cut into pieces and a bit of each is placed in the container. When things are broken up into smaller units, they become easy to organize. Likewise, as soon as an object is divided into components, it becomes possible to manage the work of assembly. The methodology of the lunchbox is closely related to the experience of organizing any production process.

In Japan both time and space are frequently subdivided. The natural features of Japan are never viewable as an ensemble. It is perhaps for this reason that the technique of enjoying unexpected sequences through absorbing things a little at a time was so often followed. The elements of scenery change one after another as their combinations are altered and

8
In Japan, each season is traditionally divided into three, making for a more delicate enjoyment of its inherent changes. In autumn, joy is found in the whisper of the wind or the shifting angle of the sun that heralds the precise transformation from season to season. (Photo: Haga Library)

orchestrated. Each instant of change is denominated and its existence yields a focal point. One travels along, or backtracks, from one to another of these areas of interest. One takes time to devour each separate vantage point with the eyes. The ancient strolling-style landscape garden is really a microcosm of the pleasures of travel in which the changing scenery is savored as you stroll. The only way to make contact with this strolling-style, travel-type scenery is by care in avoiding numerous competing essences all at once—the stealth of encountering each, one at a time. So, likewise, as one journeys about through the scenery of a lunchbox, everything disappears into the stomach.

Now if you probe further into the natural phenomena and products that symbolize the seasons, the sum of seasonal images rises to several hundred. To the Japanese, beauty has never existed outside a seasonal context. The scenery of the lunchbox is scarcely other than an expression of such a poetic. Were you to order lunchboxes regularly throughout the year and keep a careful record of their "scenery," you would discover they formulated a vivid scroll illuminating the seasons and other natural phenomena of Japan. You would thus see a revealing light cast into every corner of this intensely humanized environment called Japan.

Full Function and Conservation of Energy

Just what precipitated the birth of this enjoyable medium—the lunchbox—that features such a broad spectrum of elements? It is said to have originated in the tea-ceremony banquet style. And this must, almost certainly, be the case. The ritual drinking of tea gathered all elements of daily communication into the tea hut. Drinking tea and partaking of food are daily activities. But, into these, the tea ceremony introduced a revolution in beauty and appreciation. A fresh aesthetic renewed the texture of existence. The everyday activities of

9

The origin of the *makunouchi* lunchbox may be traced to the traditional tea-ceremony gathering. Everything from the low wriggling-in entrance of some tea huts to the limited space within possesses a density and compactness of its own. The guest upon entering is reduced to all fours and once inside finds a floor space of four and a half—or sometimes only two—*tatami* mats. The essence-of-ten-thousand-flowers is condensed in the single blossom displayed inside. (Photo by Daiho Yoshida of an arrangement by Yoshitomo Kajikawa at the Kajikawa Mansion, Kyoto, first published in *Katei-Gaho*, courtesy of Sekai Bunka Sha)

drinking tea and eating were organized into a code of manners, along with an etiquette for the use of space and utensils drawing each participant into an almost spiritual dialogue. This gave form to a heightening of existence unfelt before.

Such qualities were inherited by the lunchbox. Our sensitivities are sharpened to enjoy the sympathetic communication between nature and the human heart. In the joy of a lunchbox meal, the feeling that one is viewing scenery when one removes the lid was not a hallucination after all. It was crafted to appear that way.

This is the functional nature of a beauty that cannot be expressed in words. Functions expressed by mere words are like the greedy old men who fatten in ancient folk tales, only to be discarded by the wayside as relics of the past.

Significance of Function—The Beauty of Relationships

The exquisite skill of the lunchbox style in creating things lies in an effort to draw out all the advantages of relatedness. In the past, "function" was used only to signify mechanical effects produced in cogwheels, steam locomotives, and the like. To speak of "functional beauty," however, is to attend to the beauty in relationships of use. Beauty inevitably is a mathematical function, and there is singular beauty in the lunchbox, as in the art of flower arrangement—a technique of manipulation destined for a variety of daily situations, a beauty of combination. Augmentation of function alone is one way of developing industrial products; however, it entails a tendency toward functional hypertrophy and is not the sole option for the designer. Amplification of function is entirely different—and served to perfect the lunchbox. This method might be referred to as "functional differentiation" or "functional integration," in contrast to mere augmentation. The functions achieved in the lunchbox are legion. Were we to attempt a summary in terms of form of all the functions of a given utensil or spatial enclosure, the result would be so unwieldy as not to be of any practical use. However, it is indeed possible to avoid such hypertrophy, since we possess a methodology of an infinitely higher dimension.

A Technique for Doubling Enjoyment

Complex demands are best expressed in simple forms while remaining complex. A simple form takes into itself an infinity of complex demands with absolute composure. A sense of

10

The tea ceremony affords pleasure for all five senses. Leaf-filtered sunlight, the fragrance of fresh earth, and coolness beneath the branches where water has been sprinkled to settle the dust. Pictured is a resting place *(tsukubai)* along the approach *(roji)* to a tea house. Here the guest can have a sip of water from the ladle and wash his hands. (Photo by Minao Tabata at the Toinseki of Ura Senke Tea Ceremony School, courtesy of Tankosha Publishing Co., Ltd.)

flexible functionality has been wrought by inventing a nation of deeply greedy persons to support this sort of pattern and approach to making things. But let us stop here to look again into the lunchbox. We find nothing overly luxurious. It is, rather, the sensitively functional differentiation cum integration that by lending significance and savor to modest materials constructs an infinity of riches. This technique of proliferating enjoyment should be interpreted as the wisdom for living richly born of Japan's meager environment.

3 Equipment That Draws Out Creativity

Discovery of the Box, the Determining Factor

Were I simply to set a box in front of an overseas guest and say, "Come on, let's eat!" he would think I was joking and would feel flabbergasted or uneasy. Then, removing the lid, he would be happily surprised. All he had seen before him until that point was a black-lacquered box and a pair of chopsticks. To his eyes, some sort of deceptive trick.

Considered in this light, we find hidden here the nonconventional and unsurpassed inventiveness of the tea master. We likewise discover the lucid sensitivity to form of the toolmaker, or creator of equipment.

Actually, this box that causes our foreigner to hesitate enfolds myriad desires while at the same time serving as the starting point for a very stylish form. It was a brilliant inspiration to perceive that the absolute and typical arrangement would only be possible if a *box* were used. But why a box? Because desires are myriad and possibilities limitless, its creator chose a delimited form with an enclosing wall. A myriad of desires may indeed be set in a well-defined one-foot-square enclosure; and, having put in everything you can, the box is filled with a sense of tension.

The effect of this remarkably precise instrument of Japanese cuisine is a limitless welling up of images. For both preparer and eater, a methodology is required that is mutually comprehensible and at the same time has clear-cut boundaries. Therein the significance of the box. For whether food be arranged on large platters or in a series of separate courses, the scenery after any banquet is quite appalling. This can all be hidden away in a box with a lid. The meal can terminate with a net return to the scenery that prevailed before it was begun. This instance of "process design" is yet another of the brilliant aspects of the lunchbox.

Once the limited space of a box is established as a ruling criterion, the world image painted by the food put inside assumes an intensely condensed expression. This incisive interpretation of the box encapsulates an economy of means together with its own sense of beauty.

The Box Alone as "Oral" Tradition

Great efforts are frequently made to preserve even unfinished oil paintings. The notion of art as eternal is, after all, a Western one. In the making of the lunchbox meal, all that is eternal is the box—the artwork disappears in an instant. Similarly, in the art of flower arranging, the work is pristine in its full beauty only on the day it is achieved; then it wilts and is finally thrown away. The brocaded scenery condensed inside the lunchbox lingers as an afterimage, even when nothing material remains of the work itself. In this way, the work maintains an undeniable presence. It reappears each day with minor variations, only to be broken up, so anyone can participate. Here lies the popular aspect of many of Japan's various art forms. The fact that the framework of its creativity persists has made the lunchbox a highly sophisticated art.

Compost and Maturity

Limits are carved out of the limitless, establishing various contexts—freedom within limitations, relationships clarified through a paring away. This is the creation-sustained bound that is the physical box of the lunchbox. What brought about its discovery? One possibility lies in the fact that most of Japan's living spaces, like the paddies and their bounding ridges, have been carved out from the confines of narrow valleys. Likewise, Japan is surrounded by the sea. In this context, our country has clear physical bounds, like a living organism. This, too, is related to the question at hand.

There are few nations with borders so easily confirmed by eye. As for jars and boxes, owing to their nature, items are more often put in than taken out. In the case of the Japanese archipelago, things were seldom removed. Instead, these islands possess a "body" in which anything and everything is stored, including the cultures of other countries introduced and allowed to ferment. There has occurred a net gain in density, internal compression grows, things overlap with each other, and intimate permutations are formed. And as a result of this tacit struggle, each item or quality achieves a maturity of its own.

A Gentle Complementarity

In any organism, there are relationships of context, of significance, of role, and of cause and effect. Even though one regards an organism as self-fulfilling, it does not mean that the different components are without organization or hierarchy. Establishment of borders is common to the envelope of the living organism, any instrument that serves as a container, and even the scheme known as the package tour.

The interior world of the lunchbox works to influence the external world of food production. When you open the lid of a Japanese lunchbox and receive the visual assurance that our country's beaches are still intact and its mountains and plains have similarly escaped destruction, what you are sensing is a reciprocity between internal and exterior worlds. And it is we human beings who sense this complementarity; maker and user must both perceive it. A down-to-earth accounting of practical matters lends grace to the human heart and permits us to savor a range of such feelings.

An Etiquette of Space

When the attempt is made to convert space instrumentally, the tool-kit ideology enters in. A box is the prime example of converting space into a tool, and partition is the simplest way to delineate ambiance or mood. The character for "rice paddy" reminds us of the most obvious instance of Japanese vernacular spatial division. Gazing at the *shokado* lunchbox, it is worth noting the feeling of looking down into a (rice-paddy-shaped) house layout. The lower-right square is the kitchen, the upper-right square the bedroom; the upper-left square is the guest room, and the lower-left square the living room. This was the normal layout of rooms in a traditional four-room farmhouse, as more recently in many town flats. Rice goes in the kitchen, fish in the bedroom, seasonal tidbits in the guest room, and dumplings or vinegar pickles in the living room. This arrangement corresponds, with a little imagination, to essentials in the kitchen, pleasure in the bedroom, welcoming visitors in the guest room, and miscellaneous accessories in the living room.

The daily etiquette expressed in this spatial packaging was also developed in Japanese towns. Areas were set up specifically for mansions of the warrior class, merchants' shops, craftsmen's workshops, and for the distribution of provisions, lending a lunchbox-type pattern to the town itself. The city of Edo reflected just this sort of a complex packaging of neighborhoods, making it easy to recognize the underlying pattern.

11
The sacred straw rope *(shimenawa)* marks off the territory of the Shinto gods, a simple emblem for the delineation of significant spaces. (Photo: NNP Library)

Boxes within Boxes

Social space in Japan is packed into a box in which activities are divided up in an easy-to-understand pattern similar to the physical partitions for compartmentalizing the space of the home or city. This "box" made it easy for each member of a family to carry out his or her specific role. There were annual events held to mark the changes of the seasons, and of course rites of passage to commemorate the different phases of human life. Moreover, each rite of passage is an important step toward the creation of the *box of life*. A fresh look might be taken at the effect of such ceremonies in confirming the progress of a human life. Ceremonies, rites, celebrations, and festivals are all exercises in spiritual toning, and it would seem that each embodies an important learning process. Human beings are not very independent. As a result, they establish ritualized frameworks, partitions, and codes of etiquette as lifestyle supports. And it is equally true that when such supports are treated in an offhand manner, lifestyle is inevitably reduced to an aboriginal state. Thus boundaries have been formulated, so to speak, to save us from our own lack of independence. They have the effect of refining the scale of analysis. But conversely, such formalization courts the risk of salvaging social content as a whole and lending a conventional, though perhaps slightly bizarre and unintended, shape. In other words, if the box is well made, and the framework sufficiently well adhered to, an overdependence on form may result that hides the defects of society.

Creation in the Palm of the Hand

The lunchbox separates a world within from its surroundings—display module, as well as communication device. Foods are set out inside the lunchbox, and these communicate with one another. They speak of their origins and convey the scenery of their places of birth.

The matrix of creativity afforded by the box must always keep strict neutrality. Today the place of creativity is being warped under the guise of function. In homes and neighborhoods, all sorts of functional implements are introduced and used to the full. In place of these, a frame or pack needs to be devised and everything must emanate from its neutrality. I have a hunch we are no longer able to grasp the ways of constructing foci like the lunchbox with its panoply of pleasures, let alone the means to perpetuate a similar lifestyle.

4 Saving Grace of the Prototype

Made in a Single Day

The instant you remove the lid of the lunchbox, such a profusion of messages is conveyed that you are quite dazzled. Messages from nature; messages from the environment; a seamless brocade of values embroidered by the people; an abstract methodology; the care, skill, and style, or philosophy, of the cook; and the breath of diverse symbols and their combinations. It is truly a spectacular playing out of volition and codes. Cooking is an art of process, yielding masterpieces unsuitable for display in museums—yet with a dignified presence that everyone knows how to enjoy. People willingly consume the masterworks constructed out of a sense of beauty, with all their overtones of popular appeal. What a luxuriant art!

This technique, hovering somehow between tangible and intangible, creates its ephemeral masterpieces in a single day—however, all is not done in that one day. Constituent ideas and practices trace a long, detailed history up to the present. What is perceived at first glance may seem no more than an array of nourishing morsels from the bounty of sea, mountains, and plains. How can such a melange display the refinement of hundreds of years? This question is linked to the universal issue of how things are cast in form and shape.

Animism as Basic Principle of Form

In the background of the Japanese aesthetic of combination lies animism, or the worship of spirits. According to the animistic view of nature, deities inhabit all living organisms—including trees, grass, insects, and fish. And each entity amounts to a basic essence. There is no hierarchy among essences; they all take their place and position in one grand chorus. Without this view of nature, the order of the lunchbox could never be accepted as a single and unquestioned discipline. This order is, therefore, a physical transposition of the animistic view of nature.

12

A Shinto sacred tree. According to ancient Japanese animistic belief, deities reside everywhere in nature—in trees and plants, as well as insects and fish. Each of these entities is itself a sacred essence. There is no high or low among all these facets of the universe, for all are deities. (Photo: Haga Library)

A deity dwells in each and every thing. From this viewpoint, there is nothing that may be left out or discarded, just as there are no masters or servants. Moreover, the whole assumes the praiseworthiness of beauty.

This philosophy that recognizes a basic essence common to all—grasped in terms of horizontal relationships—is a structure that accords salvation to the most humble and one in which all things share the reckoning of responsibility. This "system" is one where all thought and feeling is mutually intelligible; where balance is achieved in the midst of opposition, and relationship is of the utmost importance. It is thanks to the intense interconnectedness of such a system that it is enabled to put down deep roots and survive.

An Infallible Structure

The stronger a formal prototype, the broader its potential variability. As long as variations are firmly based, they remain comprehensible to everyone and anyone can achieve them. They are participatory and never remain aloof. They exert a popular appeal, but with dignity. No matter how fluid, they never descend into formlessness. By virtue of dependence upon the prototype and harmony with its aims, such variations perpetuate life. Most important is staying in tune with the form and meekly accepting its power of resonance. If one submits to traditions and style—and reads the instruction booklet—one can never fail. Prototypes, traditions, styles, and instruction manuals all exist in their own right. Yet careful adherence to a prototype provides a maximal freedom that is remarkably diminished when one mechanically follows a mere patternbook. The lunchbox meal depends upon the lunchbox *structure* with its countless different styles, yet its manner of preparation is less strictly formalized than other types of cuisine. This is the aspect that guarantees the lunchbox a favorable reception—for, at bottom, the lunchbox structure contains all the latent creativity and organizational techniques inherent in Japanese culture.

The organization of the lunchbox structure is, I repeat, conducive to every sort of combination. However, this inclusive tendency makes it difficult to maintain a clear distinction between its complex, sophisticated order and sheer vulgarity.

Infinity within the Finite

Pursuing this line of analysis, we discover the road toward a refined order. With the lunchbox, we find that variation of flavor, carefree inclusion of diverse food types, and the essential inclination of the heart are all part of a process derived from the nervous system. The structure that impels us toward full acceptance is a Mahayana-type structure. By embracing this Mahayana, or Greater Vehicle of Buddhist belief, prototype of lunchbox structure, one attains freedom of choice, full use of the advantages of *all* parts, and a richness in narrative capacity. Those flowers used in Japanese-style flower arrangements and the foods of the lunchbox, as well as the rules of arrangement for both, all represent the inclinations of the heart. Here I wish to establish the lunchbox as the *locus* where such impulses are most likely to react in sympathy with each other.

Change of Appearance vs. Continuity of Approach

If we observe closely the arrangement of things, we end up meeting the lunchbox approach in numerous places. Prototypes undergo changes of appearance and style to such a degree that it is easy to overlook their presence.

In Japan our power of visual perception is based upon a thousand years of training. And thus we find ourselves quite at home with the concept of "modern design" as an aesthetic of simplicity. For the same reason in the midst of today's rather vulgarized lunchbox culture, the paddy-character-shaped *shokado* lunchbox holds firmly as the prototype of the *makunouchi* lunchbox, in spite of the fact that it is a relative latecomer. Here, however fashion and content may shift, we note the persistence of a simplified framework with *form* left up to the individual. Different cooks can easily effect changes of style, since the potential for variation is particularly strong. Yet, as the shape remains consistent, the underlying strategy merely gains in precision. The lunchbox is thus a shining example of a form that has its own etiquette of production.

The elements that go into a *makunouchi* lunchbox are generally the same as those of any other style of Japanese meal, so it is innovation that is particularly sought after. For special occasions, lunchbox meals are ordered in the hope that the more common arrangements will be exceeded in fresh combinations.

Rikyu's "Water for Tea"

As long as an enjoyment of changing styles persists, one can remain at ease. But any radical alteration in appearance would scarcely be welcomed. The range of reliable expectations makes it likely that you would never receive a weird-looking lunchbox but that nevertheless there will still be palpable changes within the realm of the *makunouchi* lunchbox. This is the advantage of a shape that adheres faithfully to the prototype, and it increases the depth of pleasure experienced. Incremental refinement in the medium range of expectations is an index of cultural depth. It was Sen-no-Rikyu (1522–1591), father of the tea ceremony as it is known today, who made the attempt to encode these medium-range graduations into a rule of sensibility. Rikyu introduced a code of etiquette serving, among other things, to avoid revealing differences between adepts and the less skilled. As a result, he succeeded in perfecting a moderately popular tea-ceremony style that focuses within reason on the prototypical. The makunouchi lunchbox belongs to the same line of development as the humble but elegant *kaiseki* banquet style of the tea ceremony. When we recognize the tea ceremony as root and branch of this tradition, we realize the magnitude of grasping fully Rikyu's genius in its permanent enhancement of Japanese sensitivity to shape and form.

5 Pine-Bamboo-Plum—Unification in Diversity

A Peace-Keeping Structure

The lunchbox structure is one, while its contents are myriad. It is a great wonder that its contents, despite their broad variety, are inevitably divided into that triple classification: pine, bamboo, and plum—the so-called lucky triad of Japanese art. No detailed explanation of this breakdown of the contents, or of their quality, is provided; everything is simply lumped together under the three headings of pine, bamboo, or plum, with no apparent rational concern for the differences. It would be boorish to question this topos.

Importance of a Mnemic Culture

In Japan, there is another popular icon—a treasure boat with seven Happy Gods aboard bearing all sorts of good fortune for a true worshiper. The genius of this syncretic seventeenth-century image lies in its gathering together in mutual compatibility "Seven Gods of Luck" who represent a broad spectrum of desires. I wonder how old a person has to be these days still to recall all seven of these happy names? Conversely, for the animistic universe to exercise its true value, each individual must revere and enshrine the names of all its myriad gods. In other words, to appreciate and enjoy the lunchbox meal, the scenery of sea, mountains, and plains that constitutes its background must be alive in the eyes of the beholder. Unless there is someone to embrace the background scenery of all the ingredients and give them meaning, their information cannot be conveyed. Culture is an accumulation of memories. In order to hear the voices of things, one must be able to pronounce the names of grasses and trees, insects and fish.

In the days when culture was still recognized as an accumulation of things remembered, thorough memory training instilled the knowledge that identified a cultured person. In basic textbooks on this subject known as the "traffic of the world," the names of the renowned products of various provinces and their distinctive shapes and containers were

14

13-16

Culture is a repository of memory. A thorough knowledge of myriad plants, flowers, insects, and birds makes it possible to comprehend and enjoy their variety. Plate 13 is the full view and 14 a detail of a kimono bearing a design of insect cages among autumn flowers and grasses, in dyeing and embroidery on purple crepe ground. Plates 15 and 16 depict butterflies among early spring flowers (fringed pinks in 15, clematis in 16) from a kimono in embroidery on white satin ground. Both are Edo period (1603–1868). (Photo: Bunka Gakuen Costume Museum, Tokyo)

15

16

enumerated and the secrets of a whole range of traditional practices rehearsed. Likewise, in the education of women and children, mnemonic techniques of oral transmission were perfected in the form of counting songs. Among these were lists of words for appraising the entire spectrum of colors, all of which had to be memorized. Sensitivities are instilled through cognition, just as cognition is fixed by memory. When strolling into the fields in spring, if you are not able to identity at least ten types of flower or come up with any other name than "butterfly" or "bee" for the many entities that flit about or crawl from one flower to another, your enjoyment of the springtime will be slight. It is only when we know something of the background of all these colors and sensations that we can experience genuine astonishment at their variety. To begin with, we must discover and admit the existence of spirits in the shape of each thing. Once this occurs, a mutual synergistic effect takes over, and the effective aggregation of deities is constituted. Man-made things must be brought into being to help perpetuate this awareness.

Power to Bring Forth Unity

If nonconforming particles can be eliminated, overall arrangement is simplified, but the predicament also becomes more demanding. In a synthesis of different essences, what is the secret of their unification? When the number of elements becomes too large, balance alone is insufficient. If large numbers of elements are forced into equilibrium, stress arises in one quarter or another. With any method other than a sheer calculation of dynamics, the lunchbox would not hold together. If strongly assertive entities are made to dwell together, their different essences may promote mutual bonding. An essence may reach outside its own specific territory and extend contact to other essences, but this is not mathematically predictable. We can only reiterate that the unity of contrastive essences occurs spontaneously.

Savoring Standards

Entities somewhat related in essence are mutually packaged to await an arrangement through bonding. This is the lunchbox style of arrangement. The important thing to note here is the sort of components that need to be set into contact with one another. When things are linked in terms of a standard of enjoyment, they go well together. This is the slightly arbitrary yet traditional standard that we find in the pine, bamboo, plum concept of the lunchbox.

Comparing Japanese-made compact cars with their American counterparts, we find that the Japanese vehicle has a greedy assortment of elements compactly arranged within, making it a brilliant example of the lunchbox structure. The car was originally a foreign import that has now become a paradigm of Japanization owing to happy changes in internal structure arrived at by combining disparate elements. But there remains something that has escaped the process. If a standard of styles equal to the pine, bamboo, and plum spectrum were known, Japanization would peak. Nurturing a unity of disparate aspects in a single modal continuity would reveal a new dynamism. One example is the lunchbox, and this same mode of dynamic structuring can be observed in Japanese department stores and shopping centers. When you visit a department store, you find sea, sky, mountains, and plains—that is, the entire countryside, and foreign countries as well. Japanese department stores are packed with daily images. Their displays are changed with the seasons. I have demonstrated that the lunchbox meal is an "art" to be eaten, just as flower arranging is an art whose appearance is modified instant by instant. Similarly, the aim of department store variety is to be consumed. In fact, is it not generally the case that life waxes beautiful through energy exerted in such directions? It is not the eternal beauty of a masterpiece but rather attention to the pleasure of each passing moment that counts here. Beauty is sustained in each instant in accordance with circumstance; the work that has been carefully built up is consumed within a constantly self-renewing canon of beauty, with its weaving in and out of both history and the seasons. Within the enveloping time-space continuum, the lunchbox structure recreates beauty in daily correspondence with prevailing conditions. And thus life and society benefit from a net infusion of beauty.

All-Inclusive Assimilation and Structuring

A Model of the Lunchbox Structure Theory

It seems to me that one of the reasons that the lunchbox affords a favorable impression is the fact that there is nothing dull about any of the many ingredients found inside. The container itself possesses a saving structure. Everything that is put inside is sure to be brought to life. This essence of the "container" can be found under a number of different forms in corporate organizations and the like.

All contents of the lunchbox are of equal value—none is of unusually great cost or status. It is a height competition among acorns, so to speak. There are no great geniuses here. Even though differences of origin are recognized, organization is founded on the basic premise that every item involved is equal in standing. There are, of course, distinctions of faction and pedigree, but these scarcely constitute a discriminatory structure. Every element is used to the full, either for its adaptability or in terms of individual merit, rather than for any specific functional virtue. It is through this sort of unspoken understanding that, in Japan, even incompetents gain positions for themselves and manage reasonably well within the organization. This is an important part of the Japanese daily survival ethic. The reason this type of personnel accommodation is possible is that in Japan plenty of time is spent cultivating human relations. Employees traditionally work in one company for their entire lives, comprising spans of two or three generations of parent-child type association. Of course, this weirlike structure is flawed and often gives rise to inconvenience. But time spent in the grooming of relationships within the organizational hierarchy offers an unexpectedly futuristic benefit in that it serves to protect individuals from the anonymity of unfeeling relationships. The lunchbox impresses me as being a scale model of this social ideal. Everything is included, so nothing loses face. Ordinary elements are united into something extraordinary. At the back of the lunchbox structure lies a long history of accommodation and integration in the relationship between different foods. And, more generally—when time is spent studying and imitating the qualities and shapes of things, terms of expression, and individuals—all ordinary things become extraordinary.

A Container That Assimilates Things of Different Character

Pairing flowers with flowers, foods with foods, people with people. The lunchbox method of bringing to light new relationships through such combinations is employed by the Japanese in everything from flower arranging and food preparation to company structure. And the principle at work here is a conviction that even when unlikely things are paired, surprisingly enough, they often do end up going well together. When the overall components of the environment increase, the number of deity types must follow suit. In Japan, unless *everything,* including grasses and trees, is envisioned together with its own deity, or *kami,* it is quite impossible to achieve any proper order. Even in the strangest pairings, order can be found depending upon the attitude taken. This is the intuition of a people who have continued to attend to all the consequences of a complex natural ecology.

This confidence also influences the way decisions are made. A general orientation is agreed upon before organizational decisions are made. And in this process, such techniques of agricultural civilization as preparing the ground, smoothing the furrow, and digging irrigation channels are widely employed. When the time for decision-making arrives, it is already harvest season, with these preliminary functions long accomplished. Only then is action taken, normally resulting in a majority consensus, the issues themselves having been more or less resolved. Instead of decisions, plans are laid in which a modicum of tolerance toward everything must be displayed.

In village councils where the Japanese style of decision-making prevails with singularity—and even more so in the grassroots village meetings—minority opinions are voluntarily relinquished in favor of general agreement. This system of arranging things, or letting situations arrange themselves, by unanimous decision is difficult for non-Japanese to comprehend.

The reason Japan found it necessary to arrive at this negotiation technique was due initially to its clear-cut environmental framework as an island nation, followed by the structure of fiefs and the other various local frameworks within frameworks that continue ad infinitum in a nested configuration down to the level of village, community, and family— finally ending up on the dining table in the legendary lunchbox structure. As soon as any action is taken, minority opinions are unfailingly assimilated. It is not that these are swept away by denial, but rather that they are reintegrated into the living whole. Unless such

17

It has been remarked that Asians accept a vast array of cultural elements, integrating these into their own cultures. We are not averse to the presence of disparate elements in our environment. Not infrequently, this results in unusual scenery, such as this traditional folk dance for the summer Bon Festival (similar to All Hallows) celebrated in the valley formed by recent high-rise buildings in Shinjuku, Tokyo. (Photo: Haga Library)

disparate elements are reinscribed within the whole, there is no place for them to seek refuge. The reason nonconformist doctrines can be proposed with aplomb, on occasion, is a belief that mutual relationships can somehow always be uncovered. Through such shifts in viewpoint, objections are abandoned and action is made possible. This works owing to an elaborate system of arrangement.

A Necessary Variety

What is the reason for the large variety of different foods in the lunchbox meal? They do not appear through mere coincidence or unconcern. Careful consideration has influenced preparation, quality, shape, and mutual arrangement. The world of the lunchbox is a perfect man-made environment based on intent and plan. This man-made environment is an *ideal* image of the familiar day-to-day environment. Since this natural world we inhabit is of an extreme density, the number of elements in a lunchbox will not be sufficient unless some twenty-five deities are invited to enliven the scenery spread in four directions under our gaze. Unless this many elements are gathered together, it is impossible to create any desired ambiance. Arrangement of this bounty lays the groundwork for a certain mood. The Japanese sensibility is quite microscopic, and our range of vision remains pegged to the scale of the lunchbox.

Breakdown and Assembly

All the foods in the lunchbox repast are carefully cut up, making it possible to put them into one's mouth just as they are. Even the rice, the *sashimi* slices, and the pieces of sweet potato are one-bite size. It has already been noted that they are thus prepared to make it easy to pick them up with chopsticks. That is indeed true. But this is not the whole story. When cut into small pieces, they are also easy to organize. The mode of organization is exemplified in the notion that because of being sliced small, the pieces are easier to assemble.

Since nature is rich in variety, we Japanese have an innate penchant for variation. Herein lies our appreciation of human character, in line with which it is considered more praiseworthy to be *multi*-talented than highly adept at a single art. In how many other cultures are things regularly carved up small enough to be handled with chopsticks, or made so light they can be held in the palm of the hand?

The Pros and Cons of Diversity

The lunchbox concept generalized to offer culture in bite-size pieces is an attempt to effect an unprecedented freedom of access to knowledge for the benefit of the general public. A new domain of activity has come into being to provide cultural nourishment in increments—in answer to a deep desire on the part of the Japanese public to devour even the smallest bite of whatever goes by the name of culture. This approach was established long ago in the world of the arts. In recent times it has spread to include academic knowledge, and it can indeed be said that popularization has entered a critical stage. It is well known that today some ninety percent of Japanese consider themselves middle-class. This may appear contradictory at first glance, but has made possible provision of anything and everything in portions that all can easily consume and digest. Most notably, fully ninety percent of the nation can now afford to buy car, refrigerator, washing machine, and television set on the installment plan—if not with ready cash.

Developmentality of the Lunchbox

Manner and Place

What can be said of the *makunouchi* lunchbox after it abandoned the formal *kaiseki* banquet style to walk on the popular side? Its attributes include a revolutionary way of dining, flexibility of venue, and mass packaging. To begin with, the lunchbox has no rules. Dining etiquette originated to make food seem tastier. But like the protocol of the tea ceremony, the essence of table manners has been lost—leaving behind empty forms. In the case of the lunchbox, it is now acceptable to include almost any edible ingredient, and you may begin eating from any part you wish. With the evolution of the lunchbox diners won freedom, subjectivity, and the joy of savoring a cuisine of exceptionally good standards. The most significant and lasting development was that formal Japanese cuisine borrowed a new shape.

Now that we have reviewed the history of the lunchbox, one more thing deserves mention: its freedom of choice of places to eat. The *makunouchi* lunchbox liberated both the venue and the "way" to eat, resulting in a new mode of enjoyment. Development invents new ways to enjoy something and, in so doing, enhances its qualities.

The Fact of the Box and Its Measurements

The developmentality of the lunchbox also reflects the fact that food is not just packed tightly inside; rather, the box is ample enough and the bits of food sufficiently small to permit deliberation and latitude in arrangement. The foods do not crowd each other, and each maintains its own shape. This is what separates *cuisine* from "fast food" in the ethic of the lunchbox.

While it is portable, there is still a desire to uphold the level of cuisine. The newness of the *makunouchi* lunchbox lay in satisfying these two contradictory demands. The lunchbox is based upon the precept that persons eating together are content to share a menu. Its resolution as a unit is precise, yet a feeling of democracy underlies it. Among Japanese dining at the same table, there will be unavoidable differences of rank, yet its capacity to

8

A lunchbox set for flower-viewing parties is decorated with lacquerwork scenes of the Edo pleasure quarters of Yoshiwara. It comprises stacked food containers, rectangular plates, and a wine flask with cups, intended for the service of a full-course repast under the cherry blossoms. Such portable packs contributed to the development of new ways to enjoy food in unusual surroundings. (Photo: Suntory Museum of Art, Tokyo)

unify is one of the hidden powers of the lunchbox meal. Though it does not go so far as the *nabé*-style meal in dipping out of the same pot, the lunchbox does indeed give everyone a sense of the same social category.

Responding to Circumstance

The lunchbox is "cuisine" that allows for production on a massive scale. If we think of the *makunouchi* lunchbox as a brilliant product, we find it brooks no error from production to distribution and, finally, consumption. As soon as an order is received, the required number of lunchboxes are filled, and as soon as the arrangement is complete, they are stacked and delivered at once. When the signal is given, they are borne directly to the conference table or other similar place of meeting in their original form, and as soon as chopsticks are distributed, they constitute the provision of a fine meal. Once price and contents are decided, preparation proceeds according to plan and is achieved without confusion or delay. Even though the contents may vary, the production strategy never does. Here is the strength of the lunchbox's ability to respond in accordance with circumstances. The familiar and efficient process quickly solves the problem of what sort of food to order for a given occasion. The choices are comparatively easy, and one is assured of a certain standard.

On top of this, Applied Technology of Circumstance enables the lunchbox to escape the fetters of uniformity. The lunchbox is popular and served everywhere, but is never repetitive or boring. Its style is always the same, but there is always something different in the contents. However uniform the production process, its results are varied. Today when the sameness of mass production is cause for universal concern, the lunchbox mass-production style replete with diversity shows uniformity need not dominate.

Developmentality of the Pack

The set satisfies visible conditions, while the *pack* exercises a veritable synergistic effect on invisible functions. The set shows its hand from the start, leaving no room for further enhancement of value. Since the pack does not do this, making it difficult to categorize, great expectations are entertained. This aura of expectancy is the key to the *makunouchi* lunchbox as a vivid expression of the enjoyment potential of the pack.

The task of arranging individual Japanese dishes for each place setting is an intensive labor for waitstaff. They must bring in vast, heavily laden trays upon which numerous small

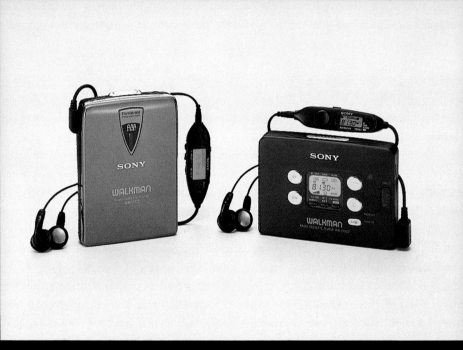

19

The original Sony Walkman was a device promoting new ways of enjoying music through the compression of stereo components into a tiny portable case. Thus new equipment engenders innovative types of entertainment. Shown here are two 1996 models of the now more-than-a-decade-old Walkman. (Photo: Sony

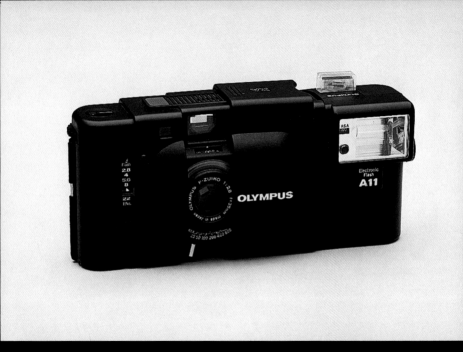

20

A masterpiece of compact design that wastes no space: the Olympus XA compact camera, 1979 model. (Photo Olympus Optical Corporation, Ltd.)

21
A simple, compact design that reveals its full beauty when stacked. The Yamaha compact stereo system Tiffany AST-7 effectively enhances a small space and creates a new dimension of entertainment. (GK Design Group)

plates and bowls of food are set. And there is also the bother of lining these up in proper order in front of each diner. The *makunouchi* lunchbox at a stroke does away with all this. The concepts that brought the style of the *makunouchi* lunchbox into being are compactness, stackability, and portability—a paradoxical triumph of convenient fit in packaging. This perfected design that holds so many hidden meanings deserves to be applied in every corner of daily life.

Pack Cities

Since station squares, city plazas, small towns, and individual communities are all established by formula and from standard elements of urban scenery, the lunchbox matrix can easily and fruitfully be applied to their design. The scene in front of the station is the face of the town that every rail traveler first comes into contact with. In Japan, wherever you go, you always wonder what sort of lunchbox you will encounter in the station kiosk when you get off at your destination. Simultaneously, you are confronted with a monotonous, insensitive, and incoherent townscape. Japanese towns today have no faces, or more precisely they are devoid of expression.

Notwithstanding the fact that townscape was once unique and thus impossible to mass-produce, what has happened to allow things to deteriorate into such a monotonous panorama? Despite the same sort of random arrangement, the lunchbox seldom gives the impression of mass-produced scenery. Where does the difference lie? To be blunt, it is a matter of poor design. For the planner, or architect, merely to line up *visible* functions, as elements of a set, can never result in a distinctive flavor, or atmosphere. Such sets must somehow be rearranged to form a pack. In Japan there already exists a fabulous system for creating beautiful things. The lunchbox meal is born and disappears every day in its millions, but the lunchbox structure is an abiding presence. In the past a related style informed townscape. Annual events, festivals, fairs, and open markets brought color to every town and district, disappearing as quickly as they had come. But they always left behind a unique fragrance and distinct air. I cannot help but feel that all concerned have forgotten the axiomatic notion that "town planning" comes before "town design." The development of the lunchbox is the fruit of a gustatory lifestyle. A straightforward procedure is essential to devise a "pack" for enjoying life. This should include an integrated plan *and* design, as well as an accepted process for producing boxes and conjuring up flavors.

Untrammeled Adaptability—Hypothetical Culture

Super-Ideology, a True Asset

There is no room to doubt that the psychological structure of the Japanese people matches that of the lunchbox. They prefer the multi-talented individual to the specialist, and even in terms of personality traits we Japanese are not easily satisfied with a single facet. It is on this account that we find it difficult to deal with such anomalous formulations as ideologies. It is a cliché that the *super*-ideology of flexible response to prevailing conditions, rather than an insistence on basic principle, is our express national asset.

A lunchbox-type mindset is gentle and massaging; it can account for everything through acceptance of diverse, and diversified, elements; and it is blissfully vague. Since each component is a recognized deity and participates as such, there is no reluctance in construing new relationships between these various spiritual representatives. For example, the land where the deity of the camera first appeared in the flesh was Germany. And Japan soon reaped blessings by inviting this spirit *(kami)* here. From the start, the camera god was ardently worshiped, Japan competing for its favors with Germany. And before long a Japanese camera god was born. This god was lunchbox-oriented so its joints were flexible, permitting it to twist in all sorts of directions and rearrange its components. As a result, all sorts of functions were added and the camera came to resemble a mini-pack. Cameras with flash equipment, electronic shutters, and automatic focusing devices that even children could use were most likely anathema to the German camera god. Only some twenty percent of the German camera ideology was kept, while the remainder was quickly Japanized. Miniature compact cameras are definitely not meant as toys and are sophisticated enough that even professionals use them. Yet in the camera world of Japan, ninety percent of all models are targeted at the middle-class consumer. Other ranges are not available. In a public with a lunchbox-type psychological makeup, a chord is struck that makes everyone want whatever catches his fancy.

Visual Cuisine

Japanese cooks are often thought of as manually oriented, but they are in fact visually directed people. Were this not the case, our chefs would scarcely have succeeded in bringing us the lunchbox, which makes the eyes work while we eat. The main concern of Japanese cuisine is layout. The reason it developed this way is likely the fact that in order to chart the complex yearly cycle of changes in nature, astronomy was not enough; we Japanese had to learn to sense the seasonal changes in our environment by opening our eyes and ears, and indeed sharpening all of our senses.

Not only is Japan almost unique in Asia in experiencing four distinct seasons, but the Japanese calendar also marks an unusually large number of annual ceremonies and events. This may have to do with the fact that the Japanese are visually oriented. Commemorating an event means making it visible, or *arranging* it. A great commotion is wrought in order to make all things visible. Converting events into icons for visual communication accounts for a large sector of Japanese cultural activity. This, in turn, affords opportunities for replenishing and confirming human relationships. Elements recalling scenery as well as the bounty of the land are lined up on stagelike altars in the manifest form of tangible products of sea, mountains, and plains. To display such items before the gods of the pantheon was acceptably the same as having them actually partake. As we know, the lunchbox meal is first consumed with the eyes and next put into the mouth. I cannot help feeling that this simple but persistent ritual reveals the time-honored influence of a feast at which both gods and humans are believed to take part.

What We Call Casual

The contents of the *makunouchi* lunchbox are a fine medley of Japanese cuisine. There are ranking families of cooks specializing in each type of food—boiled foods, grilled foods, and fried foods. The casual makeup of the lunchbox lies in its nonhierarchical lineup of foods that serve to satisfy hunger almost offhandedly. In the term "lunchbox," signifying a portable meal, one can enjoy nonchalance, yet all the while a certain dignity is maintained in the food arrangement itself. The lunchbox meal is real and tangible, albeit highly contrived, yet has a temporary aspect. Japanese culture has always occupied a domain between opposites—such as the genuine article and the article of convenience, the formal and the casual—inviting a dual structure. However impressive the reality of something, there is always an ephemeral aspect about it.

Examining the lunchbox, you realize at once that the only genuine reality it possesses is the box and its partitions.

22
A traditional New Year's Day banquet arrangement from the small city of Tendo on the Sea of Japan. Japanese cuisine emphasizes visual layout—the food and dishes of a visual people. (Photo by Shoichi Yokota, courtesy of Tankosha Publishing Co., Ltd.)

Japanese cuisine rejoices in seasonal themes, as illustrated by traditional confectionery. Shown here are bite-size molded sugar cakes, wafers, and candies served with tea in specific months of the year. Plate 23: sweets for January, one in the shape of a knot for long life and the other impressed with a straw rice bag design. Plate 24: two for March, designs of early bracken and cherry blossoms. Plate 25: butterflies made of candy and light pink wafers for April. Plate 26: candy in a wave crest pattern and flat iris-shaped molded sugar cakes for May. Plate 27: small maple-leaf-shaped molded sugar cakes and crackers with a waterfall pattern for July. Plate 28: candy in a zephyr pattern and chrysanthemum-crest sugar cakes for October. Plate 29: molded sugar cakes in autumn-leaf shapes for November. Plate 30: molded cookies in the non-traditional shape of Christmas trees and candy ribbon twists. (Photos by Ikuo Toriyama, courtesy of Japan Broadcast Publishing Co., Ltd. Arrangements by Kankyuan, Mushakoji Senke School of Tea Ceremony, with cooperation of Kameya Iori Confectionery Shop for plates 23, 24, 25, 26, 27, and 28, Suetomi Confectionery Shop for plates 29 and 30)

23

24

25

26

27

28

29

30

9   **Model for a Civilization of Maturity**

Maturity Yields Ease of Understanding

The etiquette of traditional Japanese arts like the tea ceremony, flower arranging, and cal-
ligraphy is such that anyone can participate. No matter how esoteric the inner workings of
these arts, each serves to add beauty, order, and grace to daily life. Even today, these skills
are deemed important future housekeeping assets for prospective brides. Ease of understanding, accessibility to the masses, possibility of universal participation and mastery—is
not the maturity of a culture determined by such breadth of scope? We have emphasized
how the lunchbox meal affords enjoyment to the chef who arranges it and to the person who
eats it—in equal portions. Therein lies the secret power of our lunchbox culture.

Townhouse and farm dwelling were two prototypes of traditional Japanese architecture both easy to understand and belonging to the masses. But as soon as these were converted into works of art, they became difficult to comprehend. When such difficult works
are imitated without true understanding, vulgarization occurs. Contemporary mass-market
housing designed and produced by speculators reaches beyond "difficulty" or vulgarity to
the pinnacle of nonsense. In terms of understandability, Japanese architecture has not yet
matured. It is only when amateurs are able to evaluate a work with a modicum of compre-
hension that it serves a culture capable of real self-enhancement.

Nerve-Wiring

In what, then, does difficulty of understanding consist? A failure to comprehend occurs
when our nerve-wiring, or that of nature, experiences a series of short circuits.

Man-Made Nature

We say that everyone loves nature. But nature to which people are unable to attribute
any significance or which has not been altered in some way by human beings represents a

quality, or condition, quite unrefined and impossible for people to enter into. When you take the lid off a lunchbox and the scenery that meets your eyes contains the beauty of Japan, you are moved at once by all the elements that compose this scenery—such as mountains and rivers, grasses and trees, and insects and fishes. All possess at least hypothetical names and meanings. Were they just *ordinary* mountains, rivers, insects, and fish, they would constitute a most uninspired panorama, incomprehensible and insensitive. We Japanese can only bear to look at scenery to which someone has consciously added significance. If we are to include this under the broad heading of the artificial (i.e., *man*-made), then "nature" is doubly artificial. The first man-made gesture concerning nature was the animist perception that deities reside in all things, and that all manner of *kami* journey about in the spaces between. This was an endowment both violent and magnanimous, lending nature a significance replete with fear and prayer.

By such means, the human race has continued to carry forward its semantic parcelization of nature under the tacit consent of the deities who govern her realm. The destruction of nature began with conversion into a visible-yet-invisible arena for artificialization; so began a *physical* remodeling unsanctified by the consent of the gods.

This state in which nature's nerve-wiring begins to short out here and there is retrogressive. People who have forgotten how to relate to nature have turned into a horde of unmannerly and blind hikers wandering about aimlessly over mountains and plains. Such human beings are desolate in the extreme. By contrast, nature extends an enthusiastic welcome to those who are on familiar terms with her.

The savoring of a lunchbox meal is similar to a tour of the mountains by a keen observer of nature. Fish welcome people who know fish. Rice welcomes people who know rice. The lunchbox has a mission of culinary artifice to render fish more fishlike and rice more ricelike. It is due to such artificialization that one is able to savor nature more deeply. Unless we set out to acknowledge artifice and promote it, we cannot enjoy true civilization.

31

The Japanese are known as lovers of nature, but what they esteem most is nature enhanced by human values. Nature that has been rearranged by human hands, named, and provided with a specific significance is the most beautiful. Shown here are terraced rice fields carved into the mountain slopes. (Photo: NNP Library)

Activating Infinity

We are often impressed with the physical smallness of a great person when coming into direct contact with such an individual for the first time. From a distance they appear larger than life, an aura of infinite capacity emanating like radio waves. Occasionally you see very old persons who seem to communicate with the universe; their weathered faces, too, radiate a sense of infinity. There are now electronic calculators as thin as a piece of paper and possessing several dozen calculating functions. These also give the impression of the finite acting upon the infinite, arousing the desire to hide one away in your pocket. Such new developments that shelter the infinite in the finite nowadays appear quite normal.

What is the pendulum activating the infinite? It is the organized and easy-to-understand relationship that comes from an image possessed jointly. If computers, cars, and cities were to issue from the same turn of mind as the chef preparing lunchbox meals, what splendid results would ensue. People would be drawn to activate the infinite and to seek after all manner of things—taking wheel, and converging in cities and urban communities.

As things are today, just leaving cities and communities to proliferate at their own rate is to hitch the cart before the horse. In the calculator, for example, nothing at all was left to chance. Unless an automobile, so endlessly full of desiderata from dashboard to engine, is carefully planned, the trial model comes out ugly and helter-skelter. The same thing is true of cities and their communities. Cities with no wiring scheme reveal an inevitable ugliness. A true community comprises perforce a gathering of deities, and towns and neighborhoods are places where *kami* show their faces aligned in a row. If a society overflowing with myriad deities, including all the local ones together with those welcomed from other places, were to be born in this otherwise civilized nation of ours, we can imagine what a blessed and enjoyable effect it would have.

Visualizing Spirits

A mindset content to deal with all deities on an equal footing is appreciative of everything in the universe. Let us describe a straightforward example. An English guest was once invited to view a certain great art collection in Kyoto—tea utensils and single-flower vases with their interesting distortions of shape—in short, masterpieces that had been born in a determinedly casual manner. The foreign gentleman exclaimed that these works would in

England be considered "defective." The animistic view of nature countenances distortion as the working of *kami* in which human beings are granted to participate. It seems to us Japanese as if the irrational makes an object suddenly come alive. Illogical content cannot be comprehended directly but is intuited. As soon as such workings of the sprits are "understood," whatever is *man*-made takes on especial "life."

Since ceramics are molded of clay and then fired, it is only natural to assume twistings and cracks will appear. A sympathetic familiarity is felt for the "warp" so produced. I use the word here in the sense of relationship or significance—a concept that arises from our agricultural civilization's long association with nature. The collapse of this is a manifestation of the pettiness of much modernization. Consider the tangerines grown on the west coast of Shikoku in Ehime Prefecture. These were at one time frequently served in place of Japanese sweets. They were small and strangely misshapen, seeming stunted; but their flavor was unfailingly delicious. Today, tangerines are selected in accordance with Ministry of Forestry and Agriculture standards. These stipulate that each must pass through a perfectly round hole in a board to qualify. Large tangerines passing the test are sent to the cities, and the rest are left behind in the districts where they are produced. The local people laugh contentedly, explaining that such "inferior" tangerines are really the most delicious. Nature's inner workings are thus forgotten, and we are encouraged to judge tangerines by standards intended for machine-made products. Though the flavor is lost, that is felt to be the way to do things today—a predicament indeed.

Even Bad Things Are "Good"

The movement to produce a thinner electronic calculator beginning in the latter half of the 1960s adumbrated a new notion of quality. It was sought to render the calculator both almighty in a multi-functional sense and as small as possible, that is, to establish multifunctionality and miniaturization as equal values. Packing numerous functions into something and making it smaller and thinner are contradictory aims, but one had to pursue contradiction to its limit to find a solution. Here we note the emphasis on "almighty but small," with small size implying strength, or the concept of "small but powerful." It was this sense of values—itself indicative of the basic configuration of the Japanese mind—that drove the development of such contemporary products as mini-calculators, cameras, and cars.

22

This black glazed tea bowl has an interestingly warped shape born of coincidence. It is appreciated and treasured as a manifestation of nature spirits. (Photo by Kumiaki Nakagawa, courtesy of Japan Broadcast Publishing Co., Ltd.)

Smallness and thinness—these qualities may themselves be guiding principles of civilization. Lightness betokens an aesthetic of conservation. The innate disposition that detects beauty in avoiding waste has vast potential.

A sense of beauty that lauds lightness and simplicity—desire that precipitates functionality, comfort, luxury, and diversity. Fulfillment of beauty and its concomitant desire will be the aim of design in the future. It is only when such things are achieved—small but powerful, thin but almighty, and simple yet diverse—that we attain a conservation aesthetic grounded in desire.

When modern man first entertained such desires, a tendency arose to manufacture large, thick, heavy, complex objects, with an inevitable loss of efficiency and refinement. Instead, today's shift from big-is-better to small-is-beautiful heralds a lifestyle driven by an aesthetic of conservation. Smallness, thinness, lightness, and simplicity applied to tools and equipment have yielded very superior items. This suggests an index for rating the maturity of our late twentieth-century civilization.

Mature Technology and Etiquette of Production

In the age of conservation, simplicity will become the theme of artifice for all sorts of products. But this must be a simplicity born of precision and sensitivity. It will require the most elegant applications of technology; a mature application and etiquette of production, integrated and tightly controlled.

The mature interpretation of artifice is civilization. If, in spite of a sincere disposition toward the small, the thin, and the light, one is unable to achieve simplicity, the results will be merely clumsy. In order to realize the perfect product, one must start with a refined etiquette of production. How best to make use of high technology is an aesthetic problem, while how to achieve a genuine lifestyle form is an issue of taste.

Quality, Change, and Assimilation

There is a creative bent taking things of unlike quality and rendering them homogeneous, an extremely interesting discovery in itself. In the parlors of Japanese homes of the Meiji and Taisho (1912–1926) periods, glazed sliding doors were widely made use of. Sliding

33

doors of glass accord so perfectly with Japanese residential architecture that they give the impression of having been employed for the past thousand years. But glass panes have only been used for a hundred years at most. It is amazing that, today, too, the techniques developed for exploiting heavy plate-glass, sliding doors give the impression of a long tradition. It is because of the absolute maturity of spatial etiquette in Japan that it became possible to assimilate this new material so skillfully in the domestic interior.

On the other hand, the assimilation of unlike elements may also give birth to things of quite an opposite nature.

The miniature camera was created in Japan by learning from the German model with its entirely new atmosphere. This is the conversion effect that comes from pursuing radical variants of the same product, and it appeared in clocks as well. Switzerland had for generations been the home of the clock and watch industry. Japan continued for some time to pursue Swiss precision technology, the traditional art of the clockmaker. And then just when Japan had perfectly mastered the orthodox technology, it totally outstripped Switzerland in the realm of quartz timekeepers through the use of a new crystal technology. In the process of mastering and assimilating the old technology, Japan effected a switchover to a product of a totally different quality. This generated a new atmosphere, analogous to the difference between the *makunouchi* lunchbox and the more traditional Japanese banquet style. Pursuit of quality may thus give birth to quite a different vein of production, amounting to the creation of something entirely new. This is a talent Japan has long possessed.

33 and 34

These two light fixtures in old Japanese dwellings have been transformed from models first imported from overseas a mere one hundred years ago to fit Japanese tastes. They have blended so well with traditional building styles that they almost feel indigenous. Japanese are skilled at design techniques that start with disparate elements adapted to new surroundings. (Photo by Hideki Hongo)

The Ultimate Spirit of Service—Heart of the Merchant

Masters of Action, Masters of Arrangement

The lunchbox was not originated by an aesthetician or an artist, but rather a merchant. We ought to gauge eighty percent of the inspiration to have come from the world of cuisine, attributing the remainder as a by-product of vulgarization. The ultimate aim of that merchant's spirit of service was to discover the best way to merchandise enjoyment.

In the conversion of enjoyment into merchandise, he had to perceive which lifestyle forms best fit the product. The lunchbox must contain foods that suit everyone's tastes, offer the highest possible quality of service, and at the same time be easy to produce. This is what is known jocularly as an all-purpose remedy. It was, as has been noted, a popularization of the art of the *kaiseki* banquet style, with enjoyment added, and with the capacity to turn a profit. Hence the impertinence of this all-purpose product.

In originating a product, one must have the skill to intuit the desires of the consumer. The way the product will be used, or consumed, as well as the range of ingredients, the technology of production, and the net cost must all enter into a comprehensive simultaneous equation.

A skilled merchandiser must be a master of both action and arrangement. Conferring a certain form on an item of merchandise means creating a lure that will make the customer wish to select and purchase the item. The simple design and confection of products that will appeal to the customer worthy of purchase is a service in itself.

The Art of Commerce

Service goods must reflect the desires of the public. The merchant must first grasp the occasion, place, conditions, and people involved; next he must select the appropriate product and procure it—these are the elements of any true service activity. Merchants are visually oriented, as well as being connoisseurs. They ferret out the invisible threads of the relationship that bind customer and product. The ability to arrange a "marriage" with a high possibility for success is the greatest of virtues from the viewpoint of the customer. The merchant stands as a mediator between people and things, the position of a true ambassador of culture. It is essential that customers feel comfortable visiting the shop or point of purchase. This means the merchandiser must possess astute discernment concerning the products he offers. The customer thus feels a sense of guarantee simply by making purchases at a particular outlet. All this is what makes an ideal merchant; it also makes commerce an art.

We must keep in mind that Sen-no-Rikyu, founder and reformer of the tea ceremony, was also a great merchant. The ability to judge the value of things is both an artistic and a commercial asset. Today, it is the big enterprises that are reformulating cultural standards for Japan. New types of instruments and equipment have a tendency to be poorly designed despite wasteful corporate spending on research. This problem involves the reputation of both makers and distributors. The fact that neither the producers nor the middlemen any longer have an effective mechanism for maintaining the old-fashioned dignity of mercantile responsibility is one manifestation of the bottleneck in the present-day relationship between Japanese industry and cultural standards. The only hope of salvation lies in consumers refining their perception of our daily environment—preferably to the level of an art. Daily living must be thought of as an *art,* and discernment be enhanced.

Show windows, display racks, and shop layout are all quite similar to the lunchbox structure. Products produced in different places and merchandise of different types are gathered together, and it is desirable that a relationship of significance like an invisible nerve system be established among the disparate items. However unusual the combination, if the arranger is skillful, all elements can be brought to full life. Moreover, stocking a wide variety of goods helps implement comprehensive service. In other words, total entertainment. And these are only some of the ways the merchandiser puts forward the proposal for an overall lifestyle image. If the consumer is skillfully appraised while believing that he or she is doing the appraising, the service on offer is bound to be highly successful. This is the same sort of success as providing a lunchbox meal that stimulates the eater to consume every morsel while ostensibly browsing about and choosing only things felt to be particularly enticing.

The merchant is an artist who packs and vends a lunchbox of lifestyle experiences.

A Service Activity Complex

Products are first imagined and then imaged. Technology is applied and the product is manufactured and, in turn, selected by the wholesaler and retailer as merchandise. The creator or designer, the manufacturer or maker, and the store buyer or merchant—these three members of the service goods industry dispense civilization on a daily basis.

The consumer of high quality/high value goods is grateful to the merchant for his spirit of service. The merchant himself gives the maker high marks for producing such fine products. And the maker offers praise and remuneration to the designer for an item that can be conveniently produced, then confidently marketed and sold. If the integrity of the chain is upheld, the world will doubtless be a better place.

First of all, the act of selling means the merchant proposes an item to the customer. Thus the spirit of commerce should take pride in the idea that choosing merchandise is in itself a creative act. Also the act of manufacturing must be supported by a similar consciousness on the part of the maker that he is sharing in and promoting the high art of commerce. In this context, the whole vast manufacturing-industry sector must take its place as a seeker after truth in the service activity complex.

The Way of the Merchant

It is only when the merchant and the maker work with a desire to raise their activities to the level of an *aesthetic* that the real power to enhance culture is born between them. Originally the issue of culture turned on the problem of enhancing quality of service.

Once the service activity complex of designer, maker, and merchant is established, active consumption of the product is the greatest service the consumer can render to this triad. If discernment and sensitivity are lacking on the part of the recipient, the three-member corps has gone about its work for nothing. If the product is food, the eater refines his knowledge in the active process of devouring his teaching materials. In the old-but-ever-new eating civilization, wherever it has achieved maturity, the close-knit organization requires the skilled eater, an incipient gourmet. We can best refer, then, to the service activity complex as a four-member body.

That Service Called "Change"

If the blooming of a flower be called a service, its fading and fall from the branch is likewise one. We are glad when flowers bloom and sad when they drop. Though the cycle has repeated itself for thousands of years, people still have interest in cultivating flowers. There are few types of service as thoroughgoing as this. A large share of our desires is response to changes implicit in nature. As a result of persistent response to the changes of the seasons and the comprehensive notion of change itself, people themselves are with age and experience progressively better equipped to cope with their environment. Our lifestyle comprises both a sense of beauty and a wide-ranging desire. Forestalling betrayal in the universal expectation of change is one of the greatest themes offered to industry in the future.

Revolution Is a Matter of Sentiment

Today's industry has applied thought and resources to the continual presentation of change and made use of this to refine the customer's sensitivities. Change is apprehended by feelings. In both department stores and lunchbox meals, unless a healthy feeling of freshness is provided, the service product element is regarded as valueless by the customer. Diverse products can themselves be purchased in any neighborhood shop. But we Japanese go to department stores to gain a lunchbox-type pack of reactions, to buy a sense of change.

Feelings do not modulate unless a major incident is met with. Consider the unexpected catastrophe of the oil crisis, when Japan's national mood underwent just such a modification. From that time forward for a number of years, everything was evaluated under the lens of energy conservation. In this realm of collective mood swings, there are moments when even though nothing real has been accomplished, as long as good feeling prevails, everyone is satisfied. Of course, this is a danger area.

Satisfaction of desires is the ultimate goal of service providers, just as creating a convivial mood, or feeling, is the aim of hospitality. There are moments when the general consumer wants, say, lots of knobs, levers, or buttons on sound equipment; several years later everyone seems to prefer visibility of only the most necessary devices, with all the rest hidden away. There are many similar swings in mood, even about mere mechanisms. What is the reason for such oscillation? At a given moment so many different elements are at work it is hard to put one's finger on a specific cause. However, feeling makes up a large part of existence. In order to capitalize on our rich and vivid stock of emotions, the best ambiance could be referred to as a will-to-live-inspiring environment. Therefore, a new weapon the designer might call "feeling-ology" is called for. If we search for an instance of this new "-ology" in the past, there are any number of examples. The lunchbox meal, for instance, is a pack of festive feelings, an archive of feeling-ology ready to be delved into and exploited. Could the lunchbox, perchance, offer us a simulation model in the pursuit of feeling-ology?

An Interlude

The Lunchbox Parody

That the lunchbox prototype can be applied in so many different ways has advantages as well as disadvantages. In extended formal applications, it is imprudent to forget its origins, since stylization can merely cover up for insufficient contents instead of enhancing them. This betrays our tendency to be fooled by any thorough application of style even at the expense of content. Content thus comes to depend entirely on a notion of *style:* and style allows content to be buoyed up by it. This, in turn, has given rise to a flood of fake lunchboxes or "lunchbox parodies." The very ambivalence and magnanimity of the lunchbox structure facilitates this: it makes the unfinished appear finished, the nonsequential seem sequential, and apparently relates the related. "Lunchbox-like" is an expression that seems to fit even where inappropriate, so the notion is easy to invoke in any attempt to talk oneself out of a corner. Owing to this inherent flexibility of the prototype, it would be shameful to misuse the term to the extent that the original richness and power were vitiated.

A Defense of Quality

Owing to the magnanimity of the lunchbox matrix, there is potential danger of its becoming all too easily watered down. It is a structure in which mere expediency, like the ease of filling it with food or providing enough boxes for the number of guests, thrives. Even incompatible combinations that omit essential flavors or fragrances may give an initial impression of being perfectly lunchbox-like. But if quality and variation be diligently pursued, the lunchbox will possess dignity. We must keep in mind that the Japanese people have a boundless admiration for ingenious improvisation, and paradoxically are prepared to expend infinite pains. Thus, now and always, we must be ready to stress whatever takes time—if it embodies elements of improvisation, convenience, and all-inclusive assimilation—recalling that such lunchbox qualities reflect centuries of refinement.

What is it that lies hidden in the *makunouchi* lunchbox? In Part One, I have attempted to grasp the broad array of Japanese ways of making things, the etiquette of production, and ways of solving problems—all the while training my gaze unflinchingly on the lunchbox itself. I also have ventured a few predictions concerning numerous new items yet to be born through application of these various artifices. Now, in Part Two, I shall discuss typical contemporary Japanese products and examine them from the standpoint of a "Lunchbox-Style Interpretation of Japanese Industry" in order to discover how lunchbox methods have been applied in their creation.

Lunchbox-Style Interpretation of Japanese Industry—
The Lunchbox Archipelago Today

Technology to Cope with Environment: Nature and Seasons of an Air-Conditioned Culture

Culture Copies Nature

If you fly up across the Japanese archipelago from the Pacific—the so-called southern sea—toward China in the north, you pass over plains, approach the folds of mountains, and then, just as you reach their summit, you detect more peaks beyond. After traversing this complex topography of mountains, rivers, and plains we call Japan, you find the sea again—the ever-continuing sea. But the Sea of Japan, north of our islands, only lasts for a moment; for you are soon flying over mountains once more, those of the Asian mainland. You continue flying for an hour, even an additional two, and there remain still more mountains below you.

It has always been believed that the difference in scale of the natural environment exerts a strong influence on the sense of distance and space of the people who live in these two countries, Japan and China.

I have referred to the complexity of Japanese topography, made up as it is of a number of different configurational sets arranged in ever-varied patterns from south to north and from west to east across our long, narrow archipelago. In Japan, there are any number of juxtapositions resulting from the repetition of cultural, as well as natural, scenery patterns. But each repetition contains a variation, resulting in the differences between people from the Kansai area and those from Kanto, or between people from Kyushu and those from Tohoku. The cherry blossom "front" is carefully reported by the mass media in daily bulletins as it moves northward every year, while the richly colored brocade of autumn is charted in the same manner as it extends in the opposite direction, from north to south, across the archipelago.

How different peoples respond to their natural environment influences the quality of various cultures. It could even be said that culture replicates the natural environment. Japanese culture is based on an environmental yardstick made up of things that change and others that do not, elements of scenery that are repeated and those that are unique.

The fine-grained natural environment is continually subject to modification, but at the same time it remains nature. And in response to their natural environment, we people

35
The islands of Japan support a delicately complex natural environment in the midst of which a unique scale of human sensitivities has developed and matured. (Photo: NNP Library)

36
Mankind and nature collaborate in the production of culture. Agricultural peoples who subsist on nature's bounty spend their lives in a perpetual exchange of information with the natural environment through the yearly cycle of seasons. The resultant feeling for nature is a principal aspect of Japanese culture. Persimmons are shown here drying in autumn at a farmhouse in the mountains. (Photo: Haga Library)

of Japan have rarely made any attempt to conquer or alter what is given; rather we have preferred to ensure that human beings adapt and acclimate to, and even assimilate with, nature.

To the Japanese, nature is not made up of separate parts, but is instead a complex and variously changing whole. No division into parts is permitted. Acceptance of the whole just as it is shows us a path by way of which order, harmony, and beauty coalesce for human beings.

Contemporary Remodeling—Seasons in an Age of Air Conditioning

No matter how warm an Indian summer, no one in Japan walks about the streets in short sleeves at that season, for, to the Japanese, a short-sleeved blouse or shirt looks strange in mid-autumn. But the foreigner is unaware of this. To him, clothes are to be put on or taken off according to temperature. But we Japanese dress in accordance with the seasons. With the spread of heating/air conditioning units, today it is possible to wear the same clothes indoors, whether summer or winter. Even so, we would rather match our clothing to season than to temperature.

Elementary and junior high schools, and such organizations as the police, who wear prescribed uniforms, even today act in accordance with the old custom of changing from winter to summer kit on 1 June without fail. Until quite recently, in Japan, what was to be worn when—even as ordinary street dress—corresponded to strict and detailed seasonal conventions for every item of clothing from the skin out. Clearly the Japanese prefer to bear the lingering heat or the early cold, in order to fit their clothing to the strictures of the calendar. This attitude of avoiding unseasonability at all cost is most likely quite impossible for foreigners to comprehend. In any case, the spirit of dressing in this manner is still very much alive in Japan today.

Any activity deemed inappropriate to time or place is severely criticized in Japan. Thus manuals were formulated to help people accommodate to the delicate changes of the seasons as well as to vestimentary nuances of status, or rank, within society.

Recommendations and strictures extend not only to thickness or thinness of garments, but also to patterns and colors. For example, the unique patterns of Yuzen cloth were developed from natural motifs to express the gentleness of spring, the coolness of summer, or the gorgeousness of autumn. The variety and changeability of the natural environment were thus also reflected in patterns of clothing, creating a calendar of order for proper attire adhered to by virtually everyone.

Clothes *reveal,* or portray and dramatize, the shift of the seasons. This has yielded a set of conventions handed down to us today where it lives on as a medium for making sense of the seasons—even in the midst of our air-conditioned contemporary urban environment.

The Seasons Reflected in Industrial Products

Assimilation with nature and adoption of a natural order in daily life (in what can perhaps best be referred to as a *culturalization* of nature) may be observed not only in clothing but also in all sorts of other accoutrements. For example, a distinction of seasonal usage like that of summer and winter tea bowls in the tea ceremony is just one case of the detailed seasonal order imposed even on foodways in our culture. To cite a more contemporary instance, today we are able to reproduce the effects of ice, snow, or mist industrially, resulting in a demand for new types of summer glass tableware.

In another domain, great wisdom is applied to the naming of each year's new-model air-conditioning units—machines that bear an obvious relationship with the seasons. Since we are dealing here with a piece of equipment created for the express purpose of doing away with a sense of the seasons, it is especially interesting to note the persistence of this marketing stance.

Heating/air-conditioning units are given names that bring to mind *the natural coolness of towering mountains and deep valleys* or, inversely, *warm family pleasures on a snowy day.* In any case, there is no other country that takes such pains to give suitable names to its industrial products—significant perhaps for the merging of future lifestyles with our older sense of nature and of the seasons, as we press forward into the post-industrial age. In terms of the domestic market, there are few products that can be designed and distributed without consideration for their relationship to the seasons.

Contemporary Annual Events—Christmas as Analogy

The festive carousing at Christmas in Japan has little to do with Christianity. It has been boldly instated on the calendar of annual events, once made up mainly of seasonal agricultural celebrations. Our Christmas revels could be criticized in the name of religion, but the phenomenon is best understood separately from any religious connection as a time for parties. It might just as well be viewed as one type of the annual "year-forgetting party" held

37

The Japanese people pursue pleasure in accordance with the changing seasons. The cherry blossoms are at their height for only a few days. Even today, the progress of the "cherry blossom front" is reported each year as it moves northward. In each area, people hold parties under the trees during the three or four peak days, as here in Tokyo's Ueno Park. (Photo: NNP Library)

38

We Japanese are fond of elaborating each and every seasonal festival. Here a family exchanges gifts around a Christmas tree—complete with Christmas cake and candles—in a traditional Japanese-style living room where a western-style carpet covers the *tatami* mats. (Photo: Haga Library)

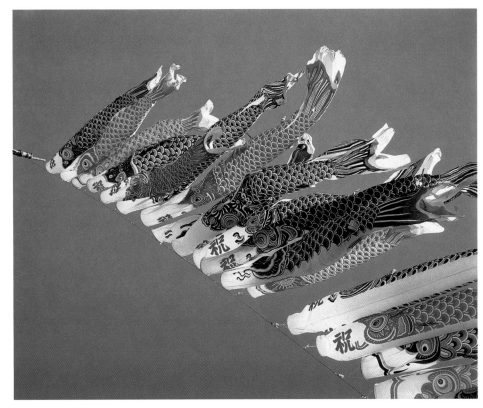

39

Visualization is a major aspect of Japanese festivals. Here carp streamers *(koi nobori)* fly in the breeze on a bright day in early summer, as decoration for Boy's Day on May 5. The streamers symbolize the hope that male children will grow up with the vigor of carp. Each fish is a painted cloth cylinder that expands when filled with air and appears to swim against the wind. (Photo: Haga Library)

in December throughout Japan. Department stores and local shopping districts have even gone so far as to coopt the name to lend a more contemporary feeling to their year-end sales by advertising these as Christmas Sales.

All this may be interpreted as part and parcel of the present-day Japanese admiration for things Western. But more to the point, the holiday provides an attractive thematic decor for banquets. With Christmas comes snow, and Santa Claus, his reindeers and sled, chimneys and mantelpieces, bulging stockings, holly, and, of course—as in England or France—traditional Christmas cake. The widespread use of such motifs for decoration simplifies the creation of a desired mood, for until some years ago there were no convenient emblems for furbishing the traditional year-forgetting party.

The agricultural ritual of sharing a meal with the deities has now shifted to the idea of a banquet shared among mortals. And it was only following this desacralization that such relatively recent decorative staging elements were devised as the stepped display for the Doll Festival and the kitelike fish banners for Boys' Day, both festivals observed in springtime. These effect an enticing visualization to replace older sacred rites now vanished.

Nevertheless, all these annual events imparted a sense of order to daily life. Those that survive still provide stages in the passage of a year, corresponding to changes in the natural environment. This is particularly relevant in Japan, where there is such delicacy in the seasons. Moreover, since agricultural ceremonies and festivals once marked the annual rites of the "primary" production industries, the older artistic and technical know-how involved is easily passed on and applied to secondary and tertiary celebrations. So by accepting Christmas as a visual embellishment of the year-forgetting party, we can discover analogous hints for the Japanese ceremonial banquet of the future.

The Joys of Bathing and Its Lunchbox Aspects

Alongside a separate space for washing, the present-day Japanese bathroom consists of a deep bathtub in which the water can be savored while warming the entire body—usually before going to bed in an unheated house. And in the not-too-distant past, this experience also included the fragrance of Japanese cypress planks in the manufacture of the tub and possibly a skylight for moonbeams, to perfect the event with a chance to assimilate with nature while bathing. The Japanese sense of practical order and aesthetics demand this harmonious merging with nature that is at the same time resonant with beauty.

Things Put into Boxes

Things not pertaining to everyday use must be stored in boxes or sacks. This represents a way of thinking common to the entire human race. Unless jewels are replaced in casks, swords in scabbards, and needles in sewing baskets, people find it impossible to sleep at night.

The stowing away of objects in boxes and sacks is an expression of fear and respect toward uncommon things, those beyond the human domain. But is this all it means? Shouldn't we, in fact, recognize a specific significance in the sequence of both putting objects in and taking them out of containers?

The placing of an item into its "box" constitutes a gesture of pacifying and replenishment, and the reopening of the "box" is an act that revives the spirit of the object and sets it once more in an active context. Something that has lain inside a "box" comes out with greater life and power than it had before it was put away. The life and care of a tool are commonly expressed by this act, bringing about its repeated "death" and revival.

Time does not come to a standstill in the darkness of the box. This is a time of resuscitation and regeneration—and, eventually, a re-creation. It is not a time of withering or decay. This is like the breath of freshness one feels when one removes the lid of the lunchbox. Such is the almost frightening mystique of the "box."

A mirror's function concerns the side presented to view. However, there must certainly be a world behind the mirror where people, tools, and other "living" things have turned to monsters and are wriggling about.

To power tools—whose very existence is forgotten when their electricity is turned off—it may be said that death comes suddenly. And, then, just as suddenly brought back to life, they work as though nothing untoward had happened.

Tools endowed solely with visible roles are incapable of life behind the looking glass. If such kinds of implements are unable to enjoy their prerogative of dazzling and fascinating humans, the human world is bereft. Before opening the lid of any container, one thinks about the darkness inside, and this instant of reflection—in the case of the lunchbox—lends increased appeal to the splendid view within. Thus the lunchbox recalls a time when tools too met with life and death (light and darkness) and a world in front of and behind the looking glass.

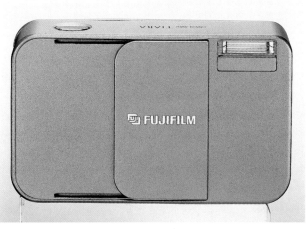

40

41

40 and 41

Placing objects in boxes and closing the lid serves to quiet their spirits. Conversely, removing the lid and taking the items out of their box brings them back to life. Traditional Japanese crafts and art objects are always kept in boxes. Each bears the name of its creator and the history of its associations and uses, ensuring the value of the piece. When the compact cameras illustrated here are switched on, their lenses come forth; their functions are awakened as soon as the covers are slid open. When the cover is reclosed, the power is switched off and they become simple inanimate boxes once again. (Fuji Photo Film Co., Ltd.)

A Contemporary Housing Prototype—Image for the Future

Westernization: From Parts to the Whole

A century has passed since Japan encountered the very different civilization of the Occident. Food, clothing, and housing absorbed the shock in various ways, and a give-and-take adaptation occurred. There were quantum differences in lifestyle between Japan and the West, particularly in the intimacy of home life, the structure of living spaces, and the physical shape of dwellings.

And it was, therefore, in the domestic field that the most concentrated efforts ensued to incorporate the style of the West, while abandoning that of Japan. Through the Meiji, Taisho, and Showa (1926–1988) periods—up to just before World War II—Western-style arrangements were merely a single part of Japanese-style homes; but, today, Japanese spaces with matted *tatami* flooring constitute only a minor area of dwellings now predominantly Western in appearance.

However, in spite of the fact that our living spaces have been converted, the inhabitants remain Japanese. There has been scant change in our deep-rooted domestic preoccupations and habits, producing an inconsistency between the vessel and its contents. Yet we Japanese are almost unconscious of the resultant incompatibility. In Western dwellings, rooms have evolved for specific functions. Normally, each room originally had a single purpose—living room, dining room, kitchen, children's room, utility room, and bedrooms. But in the Japanese dwelling, all rooms were multi-functional. Any of them could serve as a living room, dining room, or bedroom. And such special housefittings and equipment as screens or removable sliding doors and portable furniture were employed to devise any type of space required. Even today judicious combination temporarily converts any Japanese-style space into a dining room, a study, a living room, a bedroom, a work room, a sick room—or even, and not uncommonly, into a wedding or funeral hall.

A Delicate Sensitivity toward Ambivalent Living Spaces

In traditional Japanese-style accommodation, an area demarcated with sliding doors is referred to by the word *ma*. This translates generally as "spatial (or temporal) interval." In

42

People's lives require the support of objects in a living environment. Here is a design concept for living space structured by the use of movable furniture. (GK Design Group)

the feudal mansion, for example, inherent flexibility made it possible to outfit living spaces as instant offices or workshops. Closure was effected merely by lightweight sliding doors, so it was more descriptive to employ this term than *heya,* which may be translated as "room." In the delicate terminology of spatial layout, the living room (*cha-no-ma,* literally "tea space") around which daily life revolved was unique in that here multi-functionality was permanently maintained. Some time ago this traditional locus gave way to the LDK (living-dining-kitchen) combination common in modern multi-unit housing. In this context, the order of the lunchbox structure has *not* found its way into the new Japanese dwelling, where all that exists is a drearily cluttered living and dining area with visible kitchen, presenting an awkward domestic landscape.

The Closet: Lunchbox Aspects of Storage

The closet (*oshiire,* literally "push-in place") is a rectangular boxlike void inserted between living spaces. You can push in anything at all. But, if you are careless, the place reaches capacity and things begin to spill out. Each closet measures about a meter deep, two meters wide, and a little less than two meters high and has sliding paper doors. Thus, a certain strategy is required. But whether or not any real order evolves, the original nature of the Japanese closet was its basic capacity to receive any and every object imaginable. When storing small items in a closet, one must first pack them in boxes. In the Japanese dwelling, large containers inevitably contain smaller containers that, in turn, contain yet smaller containers, amounting to a spatial parent-child relationship. And in each of these, one is free to put in any combination one wishes. The dwelling is thus built on a concept of flexibility in layout combined with a further flexibility of internal arrangement. You will note a contrast between freedom, and lack thereof, if we compare the structure of a Japanese closet with that of a Western-style chest of drawers. There is an analogous contrast in the kitchen environment as well.

　　Today, high density is an urban prerequisite—hence our preoccupation with doing away at once with anything unsuitable or unneeded. We must, indeed, strive to bring about an effective and broad-ranging new economy of space—a technology for merging spaces together with a range of minutely flexible applications.

Tiny Courtyard Garden: Fantasy for the Electronic Age

Courtyard Space as Symbolic Nature

Exploring the labyrinthine corridors of an old-fashioned Japanese restaurant or inn, you frequently encounter lovely courtyard gardens along the way. And there are cases, too, when you suddenly come upon a landscaped courtyard space open to the sky as you pass along a deep veranda in an old merchant town dwelling. Or, taken into an inner parlor on a visit to someone who lives in a traditional house, you might let your eyes wander from your host's face and spy a tiny courtyard garden through the glass panes in the lower half of a sliding door.

Inadvertently, you then stop to gaze at such an extreme high-density gathering of elements. A tiny universe surrounded by walls: well-kept potted plants, a stylish clump of grass, a path of flat stones, moss, perhaps a stone lantern. A puddle-sized pond may contain water grasses and carp, or catfish, and be marked by ripples on its surface—with a one-step stone bridge, insects, and, possibly, frogs. The courtyard garden *(tsuboniwa)* contains an amazing number of such elements. It provides miniaturized glimpses of Japanese field and mountain scenery, restructured with thoroughgoing artifice as emblems of "nature."

A courtyard garden in the center of the deep and narrow traditional house was convenient both in terms of introduction of natural light and passage of air. It was also logical to bring the roofline down at this point to afford a convenient sun-and-shade angle to the eaves. Thus the courtyard garden was born of functional needs and survived owing to its attraction as a space for psychic respite. But at the same time, there would have been an even more significant ideological aspect.

As mentioned, the courtyard garden offers miniaturized glimpses of actual Japanese scenery as reminders of "nature." And it goes without saying that the means of capturing such a microcosm uses the lunchbox matrix to the full. The space of the *tsuboniwa* is completely enclosed and, therefore, independent. Thus a "box" is built and filled with "nature"; and it greatly resembles the space inside a lunchbox. This emblematic "nature" is necessary as a listening post to confirm the position of human beings attempting to live in the environment of the present. I have called the garden a partial symbol of the natural environment made up of fields and mountains, but it is also a proxy for a more universal scenery.

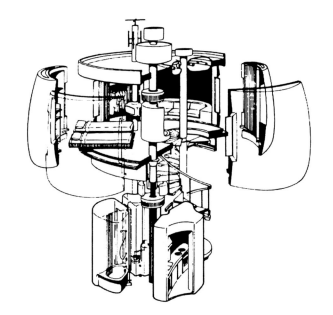

43

44

43 and 44
In this proposal for a free living space the master bedroom forms a nucleus with other adjunct spaces spread around it like an open plaza. The scheme of 1964 was named Nuclear Dwelling, or "Pumpkin House." (GK Design Group)

A dwelling is a man-made space. Districts of row upon row of deep merchant mansions with narrow-faced facades are artificial environments distanced at many levels from actual fields, let alone mountains. Thus the courtyard garden offers a significant presence in the restructuring of "nature" in such town areas.

The courtyard garden is a space that stands as staunch proof of the quality of lifestyle. It is light and shadow—heightened relief—and information. Even the flow of air is a form of "information." The flowers and insects, the turning of leaves to red in autumn, and their disappearance in winter—all these are types of information. In the courtyard garden we discover a medium for unveiling the entire universe. Here we can observe the untold capacity for change in our space-time continuum. There are forms of life growing or maturing, others just being born, and still others beginning to wither. It takes time to absorb the global reconstruction of universal phenomena in the *tsuboniwa.* Time, space, living creatures, plants, and minerals make of the mini-universe that is the courtyard garden an experimental model of the ecology of nature. It is only when generation after generation of the same family have lived continuously in a house that the courtyard garden waxes eloquent.

We should also take time to savor this eloquence. It is only after one has listened throughout the four seasons—on sunny days, on cloudy days, during storms and under snow—that one can truly claim to know the *tsuboniwa.*

Contemporary Courtyard Gardens with Artificial Insects

Today there is little worthy of listening to or spending time gazing at; and I am convinced that not a few things have been lost in consequence. We need something to make it possible again to observe our environment in detail and to gauge objectively our own position within it.

With such concerns in mind, I started to dream of a modern insect-loving princess caressing in the palm of her hand a man-made insect that had a brain and could produce the most musical sounds. The "artificial nature" of the courtyard garden is a compendium of information conveying the reality of a given environment. In the same way that the scenery of our timeless Japanese agricultural civilization is concentrated in the traditional and culture-saturated courtyard garden, the modern enclosed garden might likewise select and restructure in precise detail the essence of contemporary culture. For example,

45

This is a series of assorted sweets in plastic containers, both Japanese and Western, designed in 1986. Varied products are packaged in simple systematized units. (GK Design Group, for Isetan Department Store)

46

Here everything is arranged as unit capsules within a framework in space. The system providing for flexible placement and additions was a pavilion at the 1970 Osaka EXPO (architecture by Kisho Kurokawa, with capsule-units by GK Design Group)

growing things would be perfect man-made plants that bud, blossom, and lose their leaves in an entirely different rhythm from the four seasons we know. Meanwhile, artificial insects with eyes compounded of luminescent diodes whiz through the air. I would greatly like to design a contemporary courtyard garden filled with this sort of fantasizing—exactly as I wish.

47

The courtyard garden *(tsuboniwa)* is made up of the smallest possible units that exhibit various elements of field and mountain scenery. There are such gardens, for instance, in Japanese restaurants located in the basements of office buildings. What sort of animals or insects would be appropriate for such enclosures in our electronic age? Perhaps a micro-robot activated by light. Its "eye" is a sensor that receives light; it remembers the course it has run and can repeat itself. (Seiko Epson Corporation)

12 Technology of Order: The Buddhist Home Altar and the Department Store

Buddhist Home Altar—Lunchbox Capsule of Past, Present, and Future

A Pure Land Dwelling

The family Buddhist altar has a strange force that keeps it alive even today. Households that light incense and change the traditional offerings of water and boiled rice each morning and evening still represent the mainstream of Japanese society. And even the younger generation is sensitive enough to fold their hands in prayer in front of the altar, though it may be just an empty form for them. Given the point of view that holds the Japanese people to be essentially without religion, I cannot help but feel there is something *beyond* religion in this family Buddhist altar installed in so many homes.

When you take a careful look inside the family Buddhist home altar, you find it filled with a large variety of items. It is dominated by the darkness of lacquer resplendently enlivened with gold leaf and silver paint; it contains a quantity of religious paraphernalia occupying specific positions; and it houses the memorial plaques of one's forebears inscribed with a row of characters appropriate to the dignity of the deceased, setting them in a dimension outside of time. The brass gong introduces sound into this micro-universe; incense wafts fragrance and measures duration; diminutive lanterns shed a light that simulates movement within the darkness; and fresh offerings of fruit or flowers confer color and life. In the nothingness of the lacquered void, the image of Mount Sumeru appears to tower in the distance with clouds in the foreground. Within this artificial and otherworldly environment, an image of daily life is introduced by the votary meal of plain boiled rice, hot tea, and pure water. The drawer provided in the base of the altar is filled with scrolls of Buddhist scripture, a book in which family deaths are dutifully registered, and other similarly precious documents, making it a repository of carefully selected information. The family Buddhist altar is configured of color, form, written characters, sound, light, and fragrance—a synthesis of life and information in a finely structured, compact arrangement. Is it not amazing to encounter so much variety without any sense of overcrowding or confusion?

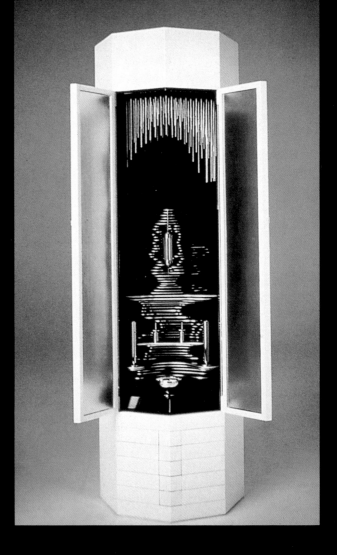

48

The Buddhist home altar is modeled on a dwelling in the Pure Land Paradise, expressed in highly [...]
form. This is a contemporary version designed in 1984. (GK Design Group)

It is said that the Buddhist home altar was created in the shape of the dwellings of the Bodhisattvas in the Pure Land Paradise of the Amida. The little altar, though it may be as large as a refrigerator, is a finely wrought and rich expression of the ideal style of life and death—appealing and apt to those who dwell in a mixture of past, present, and future. It accommodates all desires while at the same time radiating an overall order. This equilibrium was borrowed from the Pure Land dwelling to instruct human beings in unification of an infinite variety of disparate elements, which never fall into overcrowding yet stand side by side in relationships of a high density. The family Buddhist altar thus illustrates to perfection the "arrangement" method for bringing to consciousness a sense of rich abundance built up of a variety of components.

Such Buddhist altars ensconced in homes throughout Japan are accurate miniaturizations of the diverse shrines containing Buddhist images found in the precincts of all temples. By fitting this reduction of ecclesiastical space into a box, it is at once possible to carry and place it anywhere one likes. This dimension of portability gives it a methodological grace similar to the lunchbox. As inner sanctum, it represents the privileged central element in the lunchbox-type dwelling, itself capable of containing so many different things.

After worshiping at the majestic inner shrine of any Buddhist temple, one carries home a clear mental image of it—most often together with a votary token, or written prayer—to be installed in the Buddhist home altar. Thus the home altar affords religious persons the possibility of making offerings and praying to the Buddha morning and night in the privacy of their own homes. This is a markedly flexible solution. And, when balanced with the effects of being able to serve with increased consistency all the Buddhas and Bodhisattvas, we come to realize that the home altar is far from being just a simple expedient.

A Means of Communicating with the Universe

The prototypical altar layout is found not only in most Japanese homes but also in major Buddhist temples. This ubiquity is a matter of import. It derives from an ideal form, or matrix, whose miniaturizations are scattered in all directions, insinuating themselves everywhere. It is only when there is a main office that corporate branches and agencies gain significance. From this point of view, the relationship between a family's temple and the home altar constitutes the sort of system in active use throughout our society. The home altar is clearly "on-line" within a system of invisibly linked nerve-wiring.

The Present-Day Home Altar

Today our lives are filled with audio and television equipment, fixed and portable telephones, and all manner of computers. Such instruments transmit the music of faraway worlds; reveal new kinds of scenery; give off light, color, and fragrance; convey the voices and hearts of distant peoples; inform us of every sort of incident and event; and even exhort us to meditation. Information about the past, the present, and the future is stored in them. The beauty, solemnity, and brilliant coloring they project assume a powerful appeal—similar to that of the Buddhist home altar.

The Buddhist altar "of the heart" has undergone a variety of changes in different ages, reflecting the influence of diverse cultures. So, it is far from outrageous to sense the budding of the family altar of the future in the various pleasureable electric and electronic devices that today serve as mere spiritual toys. The greater the refinement the arts of design achieve, the more closely their products resemble the family Buddhist altar with its compact, welcoming arrangement of disparate elements. Here we observe a technology of order shared with the lunchbox.

Department Store as Lifestyle Showcase

In Part One of this book, I touched briefly on the idea of the Japanese department store as a lifestyle pack. These stores are normally situated close to major intersections, rising ten stories or so with two basement floors. On the roof are entertainment facilities, on the floor below that are restaurants and special event spaces, and in the basement a mass of food products. All together, the various floors provide us with every product required for daily life. Department stores sponsor special events for each season as well as at weekends and on national holidays; they provide lectures and courses, mainly for women, on everything from hobbies to general education. Thus they offer not only the "hundred" commodities promised in the Japanese name *hyakka* but also literally thousands of specialized items, just like an encyclopedia.

The department store functions as a culture and leisure center, playing the role of a vast three-dimensional lunchbox. People go to department stores to observe and experience the entire panorama of contemporary life. Total satisfaction may be had by spending half a

シャープ 液晶ディスプレイテレビ『ウインドウ』
＜ＬＣ－８４ＴＶ１＞（左）　＜ＬＣ－１０４ＴＶ１＞（右）

49

The Buddhist home altar used to serve as a "telephone" to communicate with one's ancestors—replete with a highly condensed database. What could replace the home altar in terms of information exchange today? Possibly, a flat liquid-crystal-display television set. (Sharp Corporation)

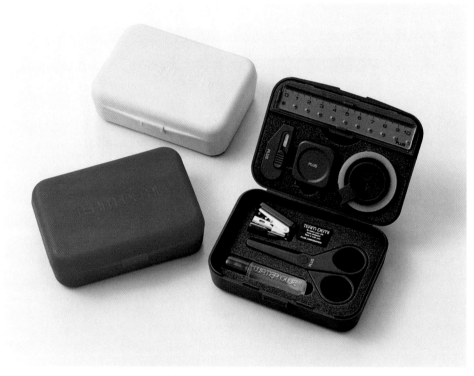

50

A superior pack is full of carefully chosen items proposed for use in the manner displayed. Shown is a miniature tool set (1984) that contains stapler, a roll of adhesive tape, knife, ruler, measuring tape, scissors, and a tube of glue. (Plus Corporation)

day gazing at the innumerable products displayed on all floors from roof to basement. Even if you go to purchase only one or two specific items, you nonetheless return home with an enhanced and refreshed image of life. Recently department stores throughout Japan have behaved increasingly as lifestyle-education marts by emphasizing up-to-date trends as a sales strategy to attract more customers. The department store deals in styles of life, and people willingly modify theirs according to what they find there. Thus the notion that if only one continually consumes the lunchbox that is the department store, one can keep a vigorous nutritional balance and lead a life of health and beauty.

In order to enjoy the department store—to create a lifestyle through it—you must take time to procure each essential tidbit, arranging these to suit individual tastes within the container you call your life. Anything still missing is supplied by the imagination, and so you are guaranteed a sense of satisfaction. Our merchandising culture constantly fabricates new images to savor and enjoy.

Technology for Quality Enhancement: Connoisseur's Guide to Soy Sauce and the Motorized Tea House

The Aesthetics of Soy Sauce

Complex Simplicity

Soy sauce *(shoyu)* is a Japanese condiment known today in virtually all countries. Both *teriyaki* steak and *sukiyaki* suit Americans to the extent that these soy-flavored dishes are found in many restaurants. Teriyaki steak enjoys its great popularity owing to appetizing fragrance and fine flavor—both achieved by simply adding a dash of soy.

Soy sauce enhances the flavor of many kinds of food; all you need is a few drops. It also has a fine, deep color that enhances appearance. It is an extremely easy-to-handle liquid and may be used with utmost simplicity for a variety of purposes. This ability to adapt to, and enhance, most foods is due to its own complex make-up—its fragrance, flavor, and color are of the utmost subtlety. Here is a model of complex simplicity and simple complexity. Soy sauce itself thus participates in the lunchbox aesthetic. One of the most basic Japanese notions about "how things ought to be" is given concrete form in a single drop of soy sauce.

Not Yet Fully Understood

Soy sauce is a product of agricultural civilization. The basic features of its production include the use of such agricultural-age equipment as the traditional hearth, the iron cookpot, and the wooden tub. These have been passed down intact in an expanded form in modern industrial soy sauce production. But, of course, as facilities were enlarged, various stages of the process were mechanized. The stage using wooden tubs was converted to pipeline; that where the fermented bean mix is stirred with wooden spatulas became motorized. And the stage where it is put into sacks to be squeezed was similarly automated. But, still, the basics of the process once used in the earthen-floor kitchen of the traditional

51
Soy sauce container for table use, designed in 1961 and still in production. The product can be used to flavor anything. It shares the essence of the *makunouchi* lunchbox in that it is simple to use despite its complex flavor. (GK Design Group for Kikkoman Corporation)

farmhouse and the resulting product have changed little. Of course, methods of chemical synthesis have been devised, but the result is never comparable to the flavor of soy sauce brewed by the workings of bacterial fermentation.

There are small-scale makers who use the chemical method, but the major brewers all use the modified traditional one. This is contrary to the rule of production for most other traditional products. Is not the norm for cottage industry to preserve traditional methods, while industrial producers adopt modernized convenience? Here, yet again, the uniqueness of soy sauce.

Technology of Taking Sufficient Time

As soon as the unrefined soy base is ready in the unfloored kitchen of the farmhouse, it is placed in barrels to mature. At major brewers today this vessel will be a maturation vat measuring several meters across. But even though the scale is far larger, the maturation period is still the same as it was in the traditional farmhouse method—around one year, or half a year at the very least. Since maturation is effected by the workings of bacteria, no matter how impatient we may be, there is nothing to do but wait for the bacteria to accomplish their task. Since any production technology such as brewing or distilling entails the presence of living organisms, it inevitably requires working in this sort of leisurely fashion. The same thing is true, *mutatis mutandis,* of most agricultural products. Any speeding up of natural process exacts its toll.

Contemporary industry is always in a hurry, so that the technology of taking sufficient time has largely been lost. We must realize that attempting to save time leads to time wasted. Yet there are cases where time is not even taken for design. At all events, the flavor of soy sauce cannot be rushed to maturity no matter how we try; in the final analysis, most people give up and wait. But what about the flavor of other industrial products? The idea people urge the manufacturer on, the manufacturer goads its salesmen, and the salesman rushes the consumer. So does this mean we must simply stop trying? The bacteria adamantly refuse to yield the flavor and fragrance of soy sauce in much less than a full year. There is a certain wisdom to be learned from the lifestyle of these bacteria.

The Calculator as a National Cultural Property

Cultivating Minerals to Promote Calculators

Sasuke Nakao is a specialist in selective genetic breeding who shocked even the innovative Kyoto School with his concept of agricultural genetics. He has written: "Consider a single wild seedling. Tens of thousands of years have gone to produce the cultivated variety we possess today. There is no way this wild prototype might somehow be instantly improved to the level of today's cultivated specimen. You may apply technology to speed up other kinds of work, but no matter how many years an agriculturalist labors and how much money he invests, such a feat of duplication would be impossible to accomplish. But we already hold in the palm of our hand a magnificently improved seedling. The cultivated plant is the greatest cultural heritage of the race."

This idea gives rise to dreamlike visions. One gets the feeling we might similarly cultivate minerals. After all, minerals occur in the ground just as plants do. I have heard that the Japanese pear *(nashi),* as found in the wild, is very small and hard—almost like a nut. But it was latterly developed into a fully round, juicy fruit. The same sort of advance has been made using minerals—may we not say these have put out the blossoms we call industrial products, which have themselves then produced fruit? There are industrial products affording an increase in human power and physical energy just as grains do, and there are others offering psychological nourishment as potted plants do.

We now have a calculator that fits into the palm of the hand. It is as light and thin as a business card—only 1.6 millimeters thick, and weighing 34 grams. People inadvertently reach to buy one as they might pluck a wild flower, in an uncomplicated urge for high-quality precision. They want the calculator because it is thin and light; it elicits the same reaction as a jewel seen and immediately coveted. In the case of jewels, ulterior motives such as hoarding or speculation may be involved. The desire for a calculator is far purer.

There is no other instance of such passionate pursuit of thinness, lightness, and compactness. Is this not something that should be inscribed as a datum of cultural history rather than the history of technology?

A great deal goes into the process of converting soil nutrients into the blossoming of a beautiful flower. But in the case of plants, there are the increasingly rare wild prototypes improved to produce a larger flower or fruit, to better flavor or color—in short, to make them into show specimens. In the case of minerals, there is no *original* form. All merely share in the same dispensation of nature. Is it not far more difficult, then, to cultivate minerals—transforming them into things like calculators—than it is to hybridize botanical species? Viewed in this manner, the finest contemporary industrial products are worthy of official designation as "important cultural properties."

The pocket calculator first evolved as a new species during the early 1960s. The seed that produced it was a dream of further development from the table-top electric calculator. As soon as this reached the market, it spread throughout the world, with major manufacturers bringing to perfection more than fifty varieties in a mere fifteen years. The principle of competition among similar products was the driving force behind the development of these many improved varieties of the mini-calculator. But this competing impulse flourished in the strange realm of technology amalgamated to aesthetics.

Tools with Brains

Calculators can be categorized: those that embody an aesthetic of thinness; small desk-top types; those for business use which do not stress thinness; specialist-oriented calculators; industrial models (desk-top types the size of a small typewriter); those set in wristwatches which are almost jewel-like; those installed in cigarette lighters; and others embedded in writing instruments. The business, or practical, calculator is an interesting category. Its major aim is operability. Conversely, the sort that is the size and shape of a bank card approaches a notional philosophy beyond actual ease of use. It is fascinating to note how such units were created through a mutual awareness of the character of the items in which they were to be installed. Those placed in wristwatches have buttons so small that the fingertips of the user look as if they belonged to giants. Since these buttons can only be operated with the tip of a mechanical pencil, the watches containing them are often sold together as a set with a mechanical pencil. They are presumably used only in cases of true emergency. There are likewise many people who conceal a calculator in their pocket, though they seldom get the chance to demonstrate it. These hidden specimens are sometimes brought out when, at a bar, it is decided to go Dutch, but usually the cashier has already figured out how much each person is to pay before you arrive at an answer. Even when you take an ordinary model along with you on an overseas trip to figure out the exchange rate

52

Precision, thinness, and lightness are sufficient to make any product attractive. The wafer-thin calculator is an elegant crystallization of technology. Shown here is the thinnest calculator made in 1979, only 1.6 mm thick. (Sharp Corporation)

53

A nearly weightless precision device expands the range of human sociability into a new realm. The AVOT is a 1986 design proposal for a new personal audio lifestyle. (Photo by Yosuke Kuroda; GK Design Group for Yamaha Corporation)

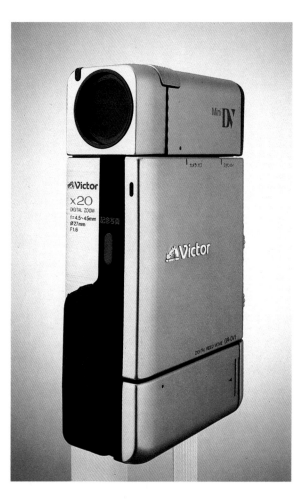

54

The pursuit of thinness, lightness, and compactness in the 1990s brought us this pocket-size video camera. A zoom lens and special effects devices have all been condensed into this 88-mm-thick camera, made in 1995. (Victor Company of Japan, Ltd.)

for buying souvenirs, you can normally figure the total more quickly in your head. All this is to say that people frequently go about searching for opportunities to *use* their pocket calculators. After all, they bought them because they were attracted by their thinness. This is roughly analogous to the casual plucking of a wild flower to stand it in a vase in your home.

Whatever the motivation, this rapprochement between cultivated mineral resources and ourselves evinces a sense of newness. Everybody has the desire to conceal one of these pocket calculators among the business or calling cards in his or her pocket. New deities are entering our daily lives in the form of everything from electronic household finance notebooks to miniature radios, television sets, portable CD-players, and laptop computers; and the way they impinge on our lives provides an endless source of fascination. The appearance of tools with brains is an epoch-making phenomenon in the close-woven relationship between human beings and equipment. It is said that the device named Mathematics Professor produced some years ago by one well-known firm is capable of answering and grading a total of 16.3 billion math problems. But the company makes it a point to specify that this is a tutorial device, *not* a calculator. The mere possession of a calculating function marks the most provisional form of pocket calculator. Today there are novelties on the market that have not only rather incidental calculation functions, but also time-telling, calendar, alarm, stopwatch, world time, written and audio response, educational, and translation functions into the bargain. The pocket calculator of the future will most likely include an even greater range of broadly varied functions in an increasingly tinier body. In terms of this explosion of all sorts of performance, portability, unification in diversity, and power despite smallness, the pocket calculator, too, has come to partake of the aesthetics of the lunchbox. It is a thing of beauty held in the hand—a highly functional and integral part of our everyday lives. It has become the first artifact in a long time bearing a genuine relationship to the tea ceremony utensils of the past.

Technological Romance—The Motorcycle and the Compact Car

Motorcycle as an Extension of Tom Thumb

Everybody in Japan is well acquainted with the old tale of Tom Thumb. A man smaller than the average person's thumb turned his physical challenge to advantage in defeating a demon and rescuing a princess. Most Japanese seem to nurture a special affection for stories

55

56

55 and 56

Motorcycles designed to possess the least weight for greatest power and function. They are beautiful because small; though small, they have power. With numerous parts into which function and technology have been compressed, such machines also manifest the lunchbox aesthetic. (GK Design Group for Yamaha Motor Co., Ltd.)

like this, in which a small but keen adversary succeeds in subduing some huge but unrefined beast. We disapprove of whatever is oversized or outspoken and despise the possessor of a swollen ego.

Judo, the national sport of Japan, can be referred to as a condensation of this same spirit. The aesthetic that considers it best to direct one's opponent's strength against himself while consuming the least fraction of one's own strength—all for the greatest potential effect—accounts for much of the cohesiveness of Japanese society.

During a time after the end of World War II, judo underwent a temporary revolution, spearheaded by the giant Heising who defeated the great player Mifune. Mifune was small in stature but very flexible. He would receive the brunt of his opponent's power and redirect it against this opponent to knock him down. The brilliance of his technique was judged to be of great beauty. Heising, on the other hand, did not have this sort of skill; rather he used sheer physical force to grab Mifune and force him to the ground. There was no error in the decision of the judges, but Japanese spectators were dissatisfied with the ruling, insisting that Heising's was not a judo of the "soft and flexible" sort, as it should be. In the midst of the shift from quality to quantity and then back once more to quality that took place in the general sense of values of the day, there remained the continued pursuit of an unchanging "soft and flexible" beauty.

The motorcycle—predicated upon the design ethic of obtaining the greatest possible power and operability from a vehicle of the least possible weight—ensured a product that was particularly apposite to the Japanese etiquette of form. The most basic aspect of this is compactness. When things are taken back to their original essence, a certain minimalism is attained. When pursuing power, lighten the weight of the thing itself and raise the power coefficient to its limit—rather than recklessly escalating the raw power output. This is the ideology of both the ancient warrior priests (*shukensha* or *yamabushi*) and the *ninja*. "Small is beautiful. Small but powerful": These are points of similarity in the design philosophy of motorcycle and lunchbox. In the land of Tom Thumb and judo, motorcycles have been produced with stress on innate skill. Such vehicles have become the overwhelming favorites of motorcycle fans throughout the world, setting them in the realm of true international excellence.

The beauty of the Japanese motorcycle lies in its expression of compact power. In its structure, exposure of mechanical parts lets us perceive their purpose and significance. In this context, elements that are nonessential or for mere show are rejected. It is through

57

small but powerful

58

57 and 58

The essence of Japanese automobile design is the smallest possible space providing [...]
driver and passengers. Model and drawing show the minicar prototype GK-0 (197[...]
into the potential of the compact car. (GK Design Group)

direct contact with a visible and felt mechanism and the resulting capacity for refined control that a new relationship of trust is born between man and machine. The romance of man-and-machine: like a "living" organism, this motorcycle revives in us the full measure of pure instinct.

The functioning parts polished with consummate skill are further purified by a dynamic visual order, integrating them compactly into the smallest possible space. Diverse lunchbox-like elements, rarefied and unified through a process of intensification, are presented in a relationship of dynamic tension. Here we sense the three elements of the Japanese production ethic—intensification, purification, and dynamism—that have now attained recognition throughout the world.

Mini-Car as Essence of Lunchbox Ideology

Much the same can also be said of the automobile. Born in this land of ours with large numbers of people in a restricted space possessed of limited resources, the Japanese car has evolved from a technology based on an idea of beauty different from that of the West. Even though its outward appearance may be similar to foreign cars', the contents are of a different order. The spirit of quality control within a limited format has been perfected in the Japanese car. The technology that makes for an overflowing tension in the little over two-*tatami*-mat space of a tea house was further intensified and purified by auto makers. Like the tea house, the small Japanese car makes the most of a severely constrained space; it enhances the joy of driving, thus ensuring the highest level of performance and comfort. As we already know, the Japanese are especially skilled at arranging spatial components in this high-density but attractive mode. A related sensibility is at work in lunchbox fabrication, interior design, motorcycle manufacture, and electronics products. In each of these instances, limited space is replete with the spirit of service.

Let us pause for a moment to imagine a future car that might take the lunchbox method even further. One such is a mini-car smaller than any current model and carrying only one or two passengers. Urban overpopulation, traffic density, and energy waste must all be addressed immediately at a global level. The mini-car is the only means to achieve mass individual circulation without poisoning of the environment. In cities of the future, the smallest possible version of the mini-car stripped of any superfluity will be a commonplace necessity.

The average number of car occupants per urban automobile trip is around 1.5 persons, with 90 percent of daily journeys less than 20 kilometers. The amazing thing is that no car has ever been designed to accommodate these statistics. In fact, more than 70 percent of all cars driven in cities contain a single occupant. This means that the space and energy necessary to transport five people are being used by a single individual. Every smaller, more efficient car will work like a yeast cell to change the quality of urban life, gradually transfiguring the lunchbox city.

The Tea House Alive Today

Condensation of Daily Routine

The modest hut for the tea ceremony appropriates one aspect of the daily round—namely, the drinking of tea—to set a prototype for behavior. But at the same time, the tea house became an intellectualized space for the refinement of sensitivities, a focal point of contemplation and beauty. In contrast to the ordinary nexus of daily life forever open and at the mercy of psychological and spiritual disjunctions, the tea house restricts its space to prevent the ebbing away of psychic and spiritual power. The result is a boxlike enclosure. Care is taken to delineate this realm from the outer world, while promoting a controlled exchange of information from outside.

The tea house, assembled from familiar materials, draws out their deepest sensitivities by sophisticated design means. Once built, it shelters such basic domestic technologies as a fire to boil water, light cooking and cleaning, and the modest entertainment of guests—a step-by-step etiquette of unification in diversity. There is likewise a concentration of craft technology and artifacts: tools, ceramics, bamboo craft, lacquer products, and metalwork destined for aesthetic appraisal. Prototypes well known within the tea ceremony and its world afford a viewpoint from which the production technology of the most mundane activities can be observed and perfected.

Contemporaneity Reveals Original Significance

The tea house reaches back to the architecture of an age of agriculture. And tea ceremony utensils for the most part recall the advanced technology of that former age. Tea came to be viewed as, among other things, a training medium for an etiquette of daily life. Thus if we wish to experience its original significance today, in the context of industrial society, our contemporary hut needs to be constructed in a manner befitting the present, and the utensils must be high-tech implements. The hanging scroll in the *tokonoma* will be a product of the latest virtual technology, and the conversation among the guests should reflect the times.

Aesthetics in a New Dimension

Not so long ago, the world simultaneously witnessed a new etiquette of eating and drinking. On that occasion the impression of the earth as "blue" was first received, as we gazed in amazement at a meal consumed in a spaceship. We still lack a tea ritual that takes this moment as its point of departure. Yet for this, the original significance of the tea ceremony need not change in the slightest. The tea-house prototype—like the receptacle function of the lunchbox—never changes with the passing of time. A contemporary tea hut must be put together by new methods that accord a fresh quality by delving deeply into the fabric and aesthetics of contemporary life. Such a tea house would persist in its basic principles while modifying only the external form.

The space capsule offers a prime model for the tea hut of the future. Tea has ever attempted to exploit the most subtle changes in our environment. Spring evenings, summer afternoons, snowy mornings—the tea ceremony adjusts the temperature of water and the height of its flame to each. Today, it is possible to have a mobile tea house that seeks its own environment and atmosphere. The passenger car has begun to alter its original aim of mobility in the direction of a media space, as if to fulfill the prerequisites of a tea house. In this mobile tea hut, there hangs no scroll, instead it is possible to view through the windshield the green of mountains or the blue of the sea. It is likewise possible to enjoy a quiet cup of tea in the midst of a raging storm, or while gazing on a broad grassy plain with stars falling out of the summer night sky. A luxurious sedan serves as a large four-*tatami*-mat tea house, while a minutely designed compact model corresponds to a perfect two-*tatami*-mat hut. The windows that let in information from outside approximate the former irregular apertures and latticed openings, and the doors resemble a low wriggling-in entrance. The quality interior appointments stimulate the same sense of well-being as in the older tea house; and, once inside, you experience the same remarkable sense of amplitude. The fact that our car of today represents and contains the best applied technology recalls

59
If we accept the notion that the tea house was made using the most advanced contemporary technology, the true tea house of today may be the camping vehicle or even the interior of the passenger automobile. Shown here is a 1962 proposal for a plastic capsule-type ski lodge. (GK Design Group)

the character of the tea utensils of the classical age. All that is needed in the way of refined attention is grace in opening the door, crawling inside, closing the vehicle, settling into one's seat, and fixing the path of movement.

A passenger car interior sets a lifestyle prototype and becomes a communication space for drawing it out. If the tea-house aspect is taken one step further, your car begins to resemble a camping trailer. This suggests purifying the tea-house capsule by disengaging the mechanical aspect. In the auto-centered tea ceremony I distinguish two major schools: that of the passenger car and that of the camping vehicle. In either case, the interior of the vehicle should be soundlessly air-conditioned; it should have half-mirror or halogen-frosted glass that converts natural illumination into the play of light, in place of the classical sliding doors and ornamental windows; it should be equipped with a ceiling letting you "view" the stars even during the day. Finally, it will be embellished by computer graphics of a complexity impossible to hand-produce, and ultra-modern craft patterns drawn by laser beam.

Today, we still lack the opportunity to experience and appraise the products of our technology, subjecting these to human sensibility as was once done in the tea ceremony. Wouldn't it be strange if the lunchbox mentality of the tea ceremony were not to be updated—integrating all tangible and intangible sentiments of our age, so these can be appreciated as everyday pleasures?

Technology of Structuring: Products and People in
the Economy / A Theory of Japanese Organization

A Lunchbox Environment Structure

Rules of the Japanese Table

The classic Japanese style of dining configures variously shaped dishes attractively on the surface of an individual tray table—where the chopsticks are allowed to stroll about among them at will.

We note the unique presentational feature of Japanese cuisine as freedom to proceed as one likes, while enjoying an overall view of the entire meal on the table. In this aspect the lunchbox meal is an exact miniature of the formal dining context. If we think of the dining table (or tray table equivalent) as a normal-sized garden, the *makunouchi* lunchbox is like a window box. But the difference between Japanese and Western cuisine lies not only in the order of consumption but also, inevitably, in the aesthetics of the table and its accoutrements. In the West, it is usual to have everything of the same design, from soup bowls to dinner and bread-and-butter plates, dessert plates, and matching coffee cups. Ideally, the silverware, including all kinds of knives and forks, as well as the glassware, including wine glasses and water goblets, should also share a uniform pattern and style.

Conversely, in Japan, except for school lunches or inexpensive inns and restaurants, there is a concerted effort to avoid a unified design. In fact, effort is exerted to provide a rich variety of *different* motifs and designs. From the standpoint of the Western chef, this is an extremely carefree attitude. But it is certainly not the case that the design and combinations that characterize Japanese tableware and its use are completely casual, for while the greatest latitude of choice is allowed, there are nonetheless a few established rules for the avoidance of confusion. To summarize the basic difference in the rules governing Western and Japanese table settings, it might be said that in contrast to the quantitative rules of the West, those of Japan are qualitative.

Since there are, of course, dishes that are referred to by size using the old Japanese style of measurement of *shaku* and *sun,* the largest plates are inevitably used as platters, which defines their function to a certain degree. Other conventions touch on the matter of shape more than of size. This allows for true unification in diversity to suit the situation. For example, there are hors d'oeuvre plates called *otoshizara* and raw fish plates called *mukozuke.* But at the same time, the size and even the shape of these are far from standardized. By contrast, the design of such dishes is best expressed in terms of an instinctive "rule" appropriate to their *direction.* For example, the hors d'oeuvre plate's shape and size are determined by factors most effective for serving a number of minute seasonal tidbits set in front of the guest at the very start of a banquet. In this case, either a bamboo-leaf-shaped plate or a bamboo-stalk-shaped one would serve to hold such a row of pristine delicacies.

The small dish known as a *kozuke* is used to serve small individual condiments. Thus since it is placed close to the guest, the rule is that such a dish be not only small in size but also of a pattern and a texture that is delicately pleasant to the touch and so can be appreciated visually. For this reason, it is considered best to employ pieces executed with superior skill but at the same time not too self-assertive.

The *mukozuke* (literally, "placed beyond") mentioned above gets its name from the fact that it is set in the center of the far side of the dinner tray from the guest. It is also a dish whose presence announces that the main course is about to be served. Here, the tactic is that it be set as far away as possible in order to play its role effectively. Both its content and serving require close attention and planning. It is thought best for such a dish to be somewhat gaudy, abundant, and thus even a bit crude in effect.

From these remarks, we note how little tangible framework there is to be adhered to; rather, everything lies in sensing the intention and choosing accordingly each plate, saucer, or bowl. As long as you hold to the realm and conventions of an accepted sensibility, a limitless range of design is permitted. In cases where the appropriate size of a particular vessel is specified, its expression and usage are generally free. Where an appropriate usage is specified, the shape may be constrained, but the design is free. In the former case the purpose of the dish must be understood and designed for, while in the latter case, it is the contextual image of the dish that must be furnished. These are the basic, if flexible, principles for the traditional Japanese table.

Skill in combining these quite varied pieces of tableware is related to the ability of the host to choose the menu, the accoutrements, and the room most appropriate to the significance of the banquet, the guests who are to attend, and the occasion on which it will be held. Here again, we see a lack of linear principle at work throughout.

In the case of the lunchbox meal, since the available typology is restricted, there will be little need to select a proper container for the occasion. Here, then, it becomes entirely a matter of choosing and arranging appropriate viands. In this case as well, it scarcely matters which food is placed in what section of the lunchbox. To be sure, there are foods that would adversely affect each other in terms of flavor and fragrance if placed together in the same section; moreover one must guard against repletion in overall visual effect. And it is this attractive devising of the arrangement that makes a lunchbox meal creative.

The sense for arranging things in accordance with standards not necessarily concerned just with appearances is also found in other familiar domains of Japanese daily life. A northern European acquaintance of mine remarked, "In cities, on dining tables, and in rooms throughout Japan, everything is arranged together with perfect composure. Traditional paper lanterns might be strung up underneath a superhighway; sofas are on occasion placed on *tatami* floor matting; and set restaurant menus are frequently made up of steak, rice, and *miso* soup, followed by coffee. The *kotatsu* I was introduced to as a traditional insulated table with charcoal brazier for warming one's feet is nowadays a streamlined electrical device. I have encountered a broad range of skill and also a lack of it in such arrangements, but I find it all absolutely delightful. I cannot help but feel this trend to be an ongoing attempt to predict the future look of the entire world."

And I, too, must agree that Japanese society is unique in its lunchbox-style environment, where it is possible to savor elements from almost any culture, in any way, or at any time you please.

Lunchbox-Style Product Structuring

Know-How Determined by Arrangement

The founder of Saks Fifth Avenue in New York once worked as a messenger boy, and he has reminisced that as he went about the city making purchases for his boss at various specialty shops, he began to think how convenient it would be to have all types of merchandise available in a single store; this is how he, or perhaps someone else, hit upon the idea of the department store—that "wonderful horn of plenty" like the lunchbox.

Lunchbox Transformation Strengthens Firms

The success of lunchbox-like department-store merchandising is not limited to the area of information-oriented products; it applies equally, for example, to consumer durables. There are a great number of enterprises in Japan that possess a lunchbox-style merchandising system through which they make and sell all sorts of different products. In Europe, where tradition is emphasized, there is a strong tendency to value the products of specialist makers. The logic behind this is a belief that it is somehow impossible for a single firm to produce a large variety of high-quality products. It is true, of course, that some enterprises rode the wave of high economic growth under the banner of diversified operation and accomplished dramatic expansion without a firm technological base. It goes without saying that a concern of this sort just as quickly loses its competitive edge in terms of both quality and price.

In the process of lunchbox-type structuring, the initial step is temporarily to set up a lunchbox-type box. But at first, it will be completely empty. Moreover, this is not a black box but a white one. When the box is in place, the next step is use common sense to avoid getting bogged down in arranging the contents. One must notably avoid any arrangement in accordance with mere personal whims. The temporary box must be filled according to a clearly defined and unified strategy. Progress should proceed in tandem: hitting on the right arrangement and devising the crucial unification concept. If unification appears impossible to attain, the arrangement will be meaningless. Also, if one or more elements are set in a subordinate position, in such a way that unification depends upon some dominant note, the result will never amount to a new lunchbox-type invention. Rather, *mutual balance* is vital to success.

In order to create a truly superior lunchbox meal, the person in charge of operations must be a connoisseur capable of probing the hearts of customers. The chef must be a connoisseur of flavor and follow this policy as he purchases ingredients, considers how to make them appear at their most attractive, and flavors the ensemble. Then it takes a cook of great skill to prepare the food. And finally, there must be an ambassador of the heart responsible for providing a graceful presentation.

A Policy Connoisseur, a Connoisseur of Flavor, a Possessor of Culinary Skill, and an Ambassador of Heart. These poetic descriptions can be replaced by Operation, Design, Manufacturing, and Sales. Or, if the product is intangible, we can modify the job titles for provision of services to Operation, Planning, Production, and Management.

Lunchbox-type products are the fruit of lunchbox-type creative processes, lunchbox-type personnel, and lunchbox-type wisdom.

Lunchbox-Style Personnel Structuring

Anonymity, Equality, and Mutual Awareness

Japanese individuals are often accused of being buried in the organization to which they belong—and *lacking* individuality. They have a strongly developed sense of belonging to the organization, so that even when they introduce themselves, they start out by giving the name of their company. This frequently happens in situations that have nothing at all to do with business. Salaried employees also tend to talk up their organization rather than putting themselves forward, and in extreme cases they appear like children hiding behind their mother's skirts. Even when required to produce a personal impression, they are careful not to overassert themselves. This is similar to the fear that the lunchbox meal might contain an item of food so large that it will destroy the internal balance of the whole.

When one of the foods in a lunchbox meal is specially featured, the meal itself changes in character—robbing it of its name. Instead, the name of the meal changes to that featured dish, such as "grilled meat" or "rice balls wrapped in seaweed." The basic principle for structuring either a lunchbox meal or the lunchbox-type organization is that everything in the arrangement remains unnamed and equal in spite of differences in ingredients or composition. The reason people inside such an organization are content to remain anonymous is that they derive a sense of comfort and guarantee of continuity.

To begin with, it is because the organization itself manipulates personnel more or less without favoritism that it succeeds in making them all equal. Of course, there remain distinctions of remuneration and rank based upon differences in seniority and ability, but these are far less pronounced than in most Western firms. It is claimed that assessment for executive positions is becoming more selective these days, but there is still a significant attempt to relate appointments to age level. Of course, in order for the organization itself to move forward, superior personnel are placed strategically; even so, there is no great disparity in salary between the ranks. This way of doing things is rooted in the aim of avoiding any form of struggle within the organization that could result in employees leaving or schism within the organization.

Secondly, this morale that has been nurtured at the heart of the organization gives its employees a decided sense of mutual belonging. Members of large organizations gain personal satisfaction in bringing about far greater results *as a group* than any single individual would have been able to accomplish.

In this maintenance of order and efficiency through anonymity, equality, and a consciousness of belonging, geniuses are rarely born. Eccentrics are permitted to add a dash of spice to the atmosphere, but it is impossible for such persons to assert themselves to any greater extent. Nor do self-centered individuals receive encouragement. For a lunchbox, as I have repeatedly emphasized, it is essential that each piece of food be tasty but that none outshines another in flavor. In the case of an organization, as well, all personnel must be of the same overall capability.

Personal Relations in the Lunchbox-Type Firm

Those who coexist within the lunchbox-type corporate scheme must maintain a sense of humility in the consciousness of forever being aided by others and likewise take pride in supporting and aiding their colleagues. Accordingly, while it is only natural that the individual is responsible for doing his or her own job well, a broad flexibility allowing for action beyond the call of duty is also needed. In order to provide this, one must constantly work to comprehend everything that takes place even outside one's own immediate assignments, schooling oneself as a thoroughgoing generalist. And in order to obtain or provide cooperation whenever the situation suddenly demands it, one must confer with all manner of persons in the organization on a daily basis—but, usually, outside the workplace—

in order to exchange information and build an understanding of personality and character. And as a channel for accomplishing this purpose, anything shared can be made to serve—same class in school, same university, same time of entering the organization, similar hobbies or tastes, same hometown, or living in the same direction from the workplace. This sort of association with others is sometimes quite time-consuming but it is of the utmost importance within the lunchbox-type organization to confirm that all are truly a part of the lunchbox contents. One creates for oneself, so to speak, a "lunchbox of associations."

From the start, the lunchbox-type organization is arranged internally in such a way that a number of different types of human materials are able to achieve mutually complementary relations. Accordingly, the personnel should not be servile types, but rather, just like the food tidbits in a lunchbox meal, they should maintain their individual qualities while working to formulate a whole. Thus the ideal employee is one who is moderately individualistic but also cooperative. An organization made up of such men and women will be capable of acting with the greatest aplomb and flexibility, somewhat in the manner of an amoeba.

In any Japanese organization, the "lunchbox" serves as the container within which anonymous personnel have declined stardom to work and perform as a group, striving above all for the improvement and enhancement of the collectivity.

The Lunchbox Pantheon

Several years ago, I happened to meet a woman in Canada. Knowing I was a designer, she told me, "I am very interested in design because I studied it at school." Did this mean that she herself was also a designer or at least a semi-professional who had a certain amount of experience in the field? Yet she did not have the atmosphere of such a person. One always has the ability, to a certain extent, to determine whether a person one meets is of the same profession as oneself. During our ensuing conversation, I discovered the truth—this woman had taken a single design class as an elective during her high-school days. In that course, she had obtained the sort of knowledge of design that is useful in daily life—how to harmonize colors, a general familiarity with the lifestyle of North America, how to choose high-quality industrial products, and so on. In Japan this is similar to what one might have learned in an old-fashioned home economics class. When you stop to think about it, this sort of class was indeed practical. Daily management in today's industrial society is dominated to a great extent by ready-made products. Such things as coordinated colors and materials, or simple first aid, are as necessary to daily life as the ability to sew on a button.

In North America, there exist a number of different styles of home decoration, including Early American, French Provincial, Spanish, and Modern. They are used for both exterior and interior, so any home lacking one of these unified styles is considered either deficient in culture or *innovative*—depending upon the overall effect achieved. Unless one is well informed about such styles and the share of the market they hold, one can easily experience failure when trying to place furniture on the North American household-goods market. Even pianos and electronic organs are likely to encounter the problem. Being more than musical instruments, they must be designed to blend with the rest of the furniture in a home.

Westerners have a remarkably high level of consciousness of, and desire for, "style." Is this perhaps a spinoff from monotheism? In any case, Westerners do their best to harmonize everything around them in a unified way. As a result, they have proceeded from one style to another in a revolutionary and progressive manner. For such perpetual revolution, they must arm themselves. It is for this reason that everything is rationalized and converted into a manual. That logic is then transfigured as a deity that seeks to conquer the entire world. This trend is notably strong within Europe. In America, on the contrary, while there is an attempt to unify one's personal lifestyle, there is little sense of trying to draw the world into line with the same style. Perhaps it is the diversity of cultures in the United States that has brought this phenomenon about.

In Japan, there is a noteworthy indifference to style. Except for the period when Japan was virtually closed to the outside world, great enthusiasm has frequently been shown for the introduction and acceptance of foreign cultures. Then, once everything that can be is absorbed, elements refusing to fit are eliminated; the rest are accepted into the general body of culture and completely Japanized. All sorts of elements have been indiscriminately taken in and related to one another. During the process, a search for logical connections is pursued, and finally, in the overall context, the imported elements acquire a new position. So there is no way that a set style can prevail with any permanence. And since this process is constantly being repeated up and down the country in all aspects and circumstances and in all places, both at the individual and national level, there is no way ever to organize people into a single expression of style.

In the climate of the lunchbox-type culture that lacks any all-consuming style trend, stylization is targeted at such individual aspects of daily life as up-to-date table settings, the way to wear and combine clothes, new modes of interior decoration for the younger generation, and more pleasant and efficient kitchen equipment. But here there are no style-based standards such as aggressively maintained by North Americans. Thus, in Japan, most everything will depend on individual sensitivities. But, in fact, it is not just due to lack of standards that the marketing of culture becomes a matter of sensitivities; rather it is owing to the fact that in Japan such matters amount to a sequence of decisions aimed at a unification of diversity, and not a style as such. Moreover, this unification of diversity is not accomplished by logic; it is only reached through training—to the extent that sensitivity can be expressed tactilely and visually. And since it is a matter of feeling, until one gains confidence through trial and error one is unsure of oneself. In the final analysis, even we Japanese come to desire a reference point of some kind.

In the past, the myriad Shinto deities put in their appearance to serve as an approximate point of reference. The master-and-pupil system in Japanese traditional arts is a pattern based on this hierarchical assemblage of deities. The hierarchy of cultural diffusion begins with the grand master at the top, and appointed teachers at subsequent levels convey the style of an art to ordinary mortals. The deities, or grand masters, even appear on the television screen. Gods of song, of entertainment, of cooking, of clothing—all deign to demonstrate and convey to the shifting masses the ambitions and aims of contemporary beauty and taste. Deities also appear in weekly magazines and as product advertisers.

These gods and goddesses mix together in a lively confusion of those selected by their Creator, those selected by someone else, those who are real, and those who are impostors. And in the words of one god of song, "The audience is god"—a sort of deification of the masses by fiat. Thus everybody becomes a god and leaves the making of decisions to each other. No behavioral paradigm could be more lunchbox-like than this.

Except for those ordering specific named lunchboxes, most consumers leave all decision-making regarding content up to the cook—who, in turn, strives to provide an arrangement of items he or she thinks will please. So this means that even the cook is, in a manner of speaking, leaving judgment up to the consumer.

We might say that Japan is the land of *table d'hôte* culture. The lunchbox meal is one example, for the *table d'hôte,* of course, is a choice of food left up to the cook—a menu of trust. Japanese, who are accustomed to this arrangement, find it difficult to deal with Western cuisine, where the consumer is most often expected to choose the dishes from a list and make decisions on how the food will be cooked and what sauces are to be used. The Japanese consumer leaves matters up to the cook, who skillfully predicts and molds the general taste of the consumer. And it is for this very reason—as also often happens in Europe—that a consumer will put his trust in a certain restaurant, patronize it, and respect it. Mutual trust among deities is the aesthetic of the making and consuming of all great Japanese cuisine.

However, in Japanese society, *all* types of work and merchandise transactions closely resemble this aesthetic of culinary choice. To do only what one has been asked is considered by us to be both unskillful and lacking in a spirit of service. But doing too much more than what one has been asked to do is not considered good form either, for it places too great a burden on both parties. It is important to perceive the level that one ought to maintain. And the receiver of the service responds with an ineffable gratitude, creating a two-way permeation at the edges of the social contract and thus forming a sort of protective membrane.

Even in the case of individual employment contracts signed in Japan, the document rarely refers to the personal functions of the individual unless the job requires unusually specialized abilities. Thus, after entering a company, the individual is often sent to a branch or factory where activities have nothing to do with his or her area of expertise; and he or she calmly accepts such a posting. The employee leaves things entirely up to the discretion of the company, and the company also trusts to the potential ability of the employee to adapt. This could not be were both not *deities.*

The Japanese thus live in a state of leaving things up to each other—in a manner similar to the harmony seen within a lunchbox meal. This is the realm in which the myriad deities dwell in mutual lunchbox harmony.

15 Technology of Aims: Goals and Receptivity in the Artificial Urban Environment

A Warning against Overconfidence

The Present Age of Planning

There are plans to cover every eventuality in life. People are forever puzzling over and speculating on goals, whether they are aware of doing so or not. The result is that in our contemporary world, consciously laid plans far outstrip the unpremeditated. Clearly, we live in an "age of planning."

As people plan their lives, they also create a utopia for themselves. Making plans is one of the most important aspects of our purpose in living, that which makes life worthwhile. And this is just one reason we cannot trust ourselves to outside forces in matters of planning.

Unconcern regarding plans can give rise to bitterness. This comes from having too much confidence in the plan itself, and a profligacy deriving from that overconfidence. One needs an extra hand for scooping up things that can find no room in the planning process or that escape between our fingers when we attempt to operate in too strict accordance with plan. One needs a "planning hand of the heart" to serve without a second thought in scooping up the dreams and liberties that cannot be expressed in words.

Take, for example, a Shinto shrine still standing in a corner of a city neighborhood that in all other respects has been laid out to resemble a checkerboard. In the shrine precinct festivals and markets are held from time to time, with numerous street stalls; at first glance these appear totally disorganized, but they are full of pulsating life. Elements like this break out of the framework of carefully laid plans and waft to our nostrils the sharp fragrances of daily life. For culture itself was originally something that could be enclosed within the framework of a "plan" made up solely of palpable artifacts, materials, and essences.

Unplanned Elements Perfect Our Plans

The cycle of four seasons and the accompanying changes in the weather furnished the original media for dialogue. Similarly, the formal meal known as *kaiseki* served in conjunction with the tea ceremony was usually created from whatever ingredients happened to be at hand. This improvisational element served to cement the precept of each gathering as a once-in-a-lifetime occasion. Guests attended such meetings with high expectations of a snowy morning or a summer's evening—and the host's corresponding hospitality.

The ultimate creativity is the laying of non-plans. It is thanks to the variety of our scenery of mountain and plain and the colorful cycle of seasons in Japan that we have nurtured an aesthetic based on unification of diversity—a culture of gentle permissiveness and latitude. As a result, we are particularly good at arrangements that go beyond the notion of planning and are totally flexible. Non-plan elements do not stop at merely providing a sense of familiar spontaneity to an overall scheme. For a plan is only perfected when it is fleshed out with certain non-plan elements. It might be added that our very lives attain a final perfection only with the interweaving of the planned and non-planned, the intentional and the unexpected.

This same genius for improvisation prevails in all traditional Japanese furnishings and household goods. Everything is set up in such a way that it is possible to arrange and enjoy any occasion in whatever way is most appropriate. The opaque sliding doors *(fusuma)* allow total freedom in the partitioning of space. The seating cushions *(zabuton)* can be distributed freely in number and position. And then there is the wind bell *(furin)* that waves about, tinkling with the slightest breeze in summer. It is on the strength of these improvisational Japanese furnishings that the people of Japan have based the refinement of their sensitivities in order to provide for the expression of a modest humanity, warmth, and a sense of occasion. Provisions linked to time and place work to convey the host's intentions throughout the space of gathering.

In planning at all levels, including urban plans, regional plans, and those for municipal building, the process ought not to start with a hasty image of the completed form, but rather thought should be concentrated on giving form to the gradual stages of realization. Humble, patient waiting for the birth of whatever should be born is the proper spirit in which to bring forth true results. Only when we speak of aims do we begin to get a sense of watching plans mature spontaneously.

However, such a non-plan can only be accomplished with a plan behind it. Diversity is achieved when we start from a premise of consistency; improvisation achieves form when based upon estimates. The important thing here is to avoid *overstating* plans and hence to approach the setting up of plans with an implicit understanding that the final result is likely to surpass the framework of the plan itself, merging with a state of nature.

Nucleus of a New City—Role of the Artificial Infrastructure

Roads—or Buildings?

High-rise buildings are aligned in a row, and at about the third-floor level, an artificial promenade deck has been constructed to fill the space between and link these buildings with one another. During the day, people relax on benches surrounded by flower beds, while others enjoy just strolling about. Below are open-air restaurants with umbrellas over each table, and cars etch out parabolas under a pedestrian bridge, as they drive into the subterranean parking garage.

Recently this sort of man-made cityscape has begun to appear here and there throughout Japan. Space is partitioned into a number of levels for different activities. Such infrastructures give the impression of being part of the traffic pattern as well as extensions of surrounding buildings. But this man-made scenery belongs neither to streets nor to buildings—it can best be called a third element of the urban infrastructure devised as a solution to the various problems faced today by our cities.

Problems Born of the City

Comparison is often made between cities and the human body. In past times the urban structure, or its skeleton, was never the object of conscious planning, but was instead allowed to develop naturally. This has given rise to a certain confusion of aims, preventing the maturation of urban development beyond a certain point. As a result, disorganized and distorted development spawned such problems as environmental pollution, chronic difficulty of obtaining land, and a reduction in the size and quality of housing.

And it is not only the central areas of cities that are in trouble. If we shift our gaze to the suburbs, we find every piece of land covered with sprawling housing. Congestion and lack of parking facilities vitiate the conventional role of streets and pedestrian spaces, making it impossible even for vehicles to fulfill their original function. Also, commuting times and distances well beyond acceptable norms cause serious loss to society as a whole. This can best be accounted for as a social cost of undisciplined urban development.

The Meaning of Development

The major goal of man-made infrastructures is the creation of a new urban nucleus. Such nuclei are normally grafted onto the existing traffic network and centered on business and commercial functions. The countless shopping areas situated around train stations throughout Japan also form urban nuclei—places of meeting and parting—for persons, goods, and information.

This type of urban nucleus also developed naturally and fulfilled similar functions in the past—multi-functional facilities making up the scenery surrounding virtually any train station. People's desires and the focus of their interests brilliantly expressed in terms of color, form, and light were converted into a living and breathing presence. Their mutual comings and goings, in which all participate unselfconsciously, created a vigorous and pleasant whirlpool of activity centered on the station.

But these naturally generated nuclei soon came to witness such hazards as fires and traffic accidents that result from overcrowding and poor arrangement, not to speak of inefficient land use. The advantages of today's man-made infrastructural redevelopment lie not only in the provision of an immediately superior environment for development, but also in the ability of such complexes to play the role of a nodal subsystem within the context of the overall urban scheme. All this is well expressed in the traffic organization of the infrastructural node, for one of its major purposes is to facilitate a smooth circulation of people, goods, and activities through separation into functional flow groups. A related example would be the skyway system that has been used with such success to connect downtown buildings in the United States, in such cities as Cincinnati and Minneapolis.

The man-made infrastructure may be compared to the lunchbox. The items introduced depend on the general conditions of circulation, in the context of which the city's chefs insert and arrange the contents to their own tastes. And it is the role of the infrastructural designer to establish a mechanism comparable to the +-shaped cross partition of the *shokado* lunchbox.

Conditions of the Lunchbox City

We Japanese have always preferred an overcrowded, bustling atmosphere in our cities, if only because this makes it possible to carry out most daily activities satisfactorily within a small radius—a sort of cultural background, it may be noted, is also at work here. It is for this reason that when we build underground shopping malls in Japan they all tend to resemble each other, and these differ from those American high-rise buildings filled only with offices.

In the Japanese city, there is no single controlling center, no structure that focuses every activity around itself. There are always at least four or five subcenters, as well as numerous other *sub*-subcenters. There is one surrounding every station, mainline or local. Each includes a complex set of facilities for procuring the necessities of daily life—greengrocers, fish shops, bars and pubs, restaurants, real estate agencies, and banks. Any Japanese metropolis is made up of a large number of these greater or lesser nuclei, or city centers. In fact, Tokyo was originally created as an agglomeration of villages, so it is only natural that on occasion it is still referred to as the world's largest village. Those many villages have long since joined together, sometimes colliding with each other like ripples and at other times yielding a simple boundary, all in all formulating an environment of an extreme high density.

Lunchbox Cities of Japan

Tokyo, however, is not the only place where myriad deities abide; they inhabit all other Japanese cities. And these, too, with their complex social, cultural, and environmental infrastructures, have for centuries supported a burgeoning population, absorbed and assimilated the bombardment of foreign influences, and helped ensure a national resiliency. This urban texture on a national scale with its countless options is a sophisticated lunchbox matrix. Should it prove possible to create an urban environment where each city center has its own individual complexion, where an order agreeable to all is restored, and where everyone lives close to their workplace—eliminating the great daily flux from the suburbs—we could then enjoy marvelous lunchbox cities everywhere, and even a *global* lunchbox community.

Lifestyle Technology: Shaping Human Character and the Ideal of the Single Blossom

The Future of Education

In Japan, from elementary school through the first two years of university, all education is general, with care taken to avoid concentration in any single field. The curriculum is lunchbox-like, but the structure is quite *un*-lunchbox-like owing to its overall discontinuity and mutual irrelevance. Instruction in the basic elements of almost all areas of human knowledge is good in itself; the problem today is insufficient motivation to ingest that knowledge.

Our education is focused on an entrance exam system in which everything swallowed must be spit out just as taken in, offering the student absolutely no latitude for savoring the inherent colors and fragrances of various intellectual domains. Originally, learning required that every student attain a sense of the unique flavors of each subject. It was through such savoring that, in a best-case scenario, one chose a specialty to be pursued in university and afterward. Under present conditions, a vast assemblage of unrelated chunks of raw knowledge serves to determine entrance qualifications, while special fields of study are deduced from the relative level of competence shown by each student. Knowledge aimed at passing examinations loses its value the moment evaluation is complete.

Spiritual Intellect vs. Physical Intellect

In the past we Japanese considered it necessary for a person however physically small to be agile, sensitive, and able. Everyone wished to impress as being "bright and outstanding" in spite of physical stature. Among traditional legends, there is one similar to the earlier-mentioned Tom Thumb, about a small boy named Ushiwaka. Using only an iron battle fan, Ushiwaka engaged the formidable warrior Benkei armed with seven weapons. Benkei attacked with each weapon in turn, but Ushiwaka was finally able to catch Benkei off guard and smite him with his fan. In the end, Benkei was so weighted down by his numerous weapons that he lost to the lightly armed Ushiwaka. This is an ancient legend that high-lights the designer's rational simplification of diversity and synthesis of function. The Mitsubishi Zero fighter plane of World War II fame was forged from the Ushiwaka proto-type. This sort of functional strategy was more intellectual than spiritual.

Present-day education has completely robbed Japanese youth of this highly desirable psychological and physical mobility. Not so long ago, it was our animal agility, lucidity, and instinct that served to motivate a straightforward sense of beauty. Our innate dexter-ity gave the impression that even the fingers possessed intellect. Countless such intelligent fingers long supported Japan's traditional handicrafts and also served to establish our more recent electronics industry. These same fingers of intellect nurtured the indispensable relation between hands and tools, making it possible to handle chopsticks or to secure the knotted cloth wrapper known as the *furoshiki*. These are points that must not be missed in the balanced education of an entire individual. It is only when spiritual intelligence joins with physical intelligence that beauty of form is born. The beauty of the lunchbox was not achieved by mere concepts; through the chef's physical skill, a spiritual intellect was brought into play and crystallized as beauty.

Understanding What Is Different

The different peoples of the earth all have their unique ways of looking at things, so today's world is still a place where numerous senses of value coexist. And it is through the exercise of our various overlapping psychologies that we are able to cooperate with those quite unlike ourselves, eliciting unification-of-diversity responses from one another. Nurturing a spirit of acceptance is one of the great challenges faced by education in our world today.

A Lunchbox-Style Theory of Civilization

What Is Progress?

Groups engage in responding to or shaping their environment, with civilization the prod-uct or sum total of such activity. It is said that we cannot dispute the progress of civiliza-tion, but we can certainly talk about it. But in such discussions progress takes on an image of logical or rational movement toward a goal. We rarely think about the blend of all that has originated in different ages. In Japan, there is no end of seemingly contradictory examples, such as the quite usual blessing of a high-rise building site by a Shinto priest. Thus the most overworked model of cultural criticism is to point out the radical conjunction of Japanese and Western lifestyles since the end of World War II. But is it not true that even traditional Japanese civilization was always nurtured through the appropriation of bits and pieces of all manner of foreign cultures? Nonetheless, the era of taking Western Europe as a paradigm while maintaining one's critical distance from it is long past.

Japanese society consists of numerous strata of values retained from different sources—an amalgamation of disparate cultural elements, or rather a mosaic where odds and ends are crowded up against each other. Most of us sense no contradiction or confusion, for supported by instinct and curiosity, we have long made free with these disparate elements, selecting those that are most congenial. And the result of this total freedom of choice *is* today's Japan.

An Age of Regions

Tokyo is an indisputable microcosm. Foreigners never call Tokyo beautiful, but many of them speak of it as an interesting capital. Anything there is to see, eat, or wear abroad can be bought or experienced in Tokyo. In addition, anything and everything from all over Japan can also be had in Tokyo. And this is the source of the city's interest and vigor. Even in the days when it was called Edo, Tokyo already assured limitless variety and vitality. Today, as long as regions outside the capital keep their uniqueness, it is possible for Tokyo to maintain its allure. But if all regional towns and cities should themselves turn into Little Tokyos, Japan will be reduced to dreary homogeneity.

Recently there has been a fair amount of talk about the "arrival of an age of regions," and such would perhaps be only natural. For as long as Tokyo monopolizes politics, economics, and art, the old, varied cultural vocabulary will progressively weaken. However, the panoply of items in the lunchbox creates a lively scenery thanks to their true variety and not to any bogus "regionalism" invented by bureaucrats.

60

The façade of an old town dwelling is a simple construction of abstract lines tolerating the coexistence of various elements. The quintessential Japanese sense of form comprises numerous disparate shapes and rhythms. (Photo: Haga Library)

Japan's Information Era

The information-intensive society subverts all values. An infinite relativity prevails and it is difficult to discover the genuine self-confidence of an original lifestyle. This flood of information places demands on each of us to acquire adaptability. Selection of only the most desirable information may be one such technique; another is to sift information through face-to-face conversations and interviews. Japanese culture is predisposed to absorb the surge of new information like a sponge. But exactly where and in what age did this spongelike disposition most successfully show itself? Was it in the Katsura Detached Palace, or in the Toshogu Shrine at Nikko, or in the ancient times of the Manyo poetry anthology, or during the flashy Genroku era of Edo? But what we are really asking is whether a *true* Japanese culture ever existed. Self-evidently, our culture has established various values where appropriate. It may be best compared to the infinity of lines in the palm of the hand. The struggle among conflicting values eventually settles into its proper place. There is neither genealogy nor evolution nor hierarchy setting one above another, rather everything is left up to human choices. It may be said that Japanese society affords countless channels for promoting selection.

Pockets of Culture

Ours is a controlled society, one in which people ceaselessly emphasize and enforce mutual dependence of behavior. Individual actions are preempted by society, leaving scarce leeway for personal initiative. Yet, while Japanese society moves implacably toward the goal of social determinism, there remains a casting about among all sorts of values. Thus confronting a pool of diverse values, we allow various methods of choice. And this is what creates the suppleness of our social fabric—what may best be called an elastic economy of structure. But in America's contemporary industrial and marketing goals, there is no mature culture of choice—there is nothing but a culture of youth. Even the elderly are required to conform with standards of youth.

The faces of the U.S. senior population are clouded by their determination to follow the quest of youth and by a lonely sadness in the knowledge that the way is closed to them. Since society has indeed aged, we need not only a senior culture but a children's culture and a women's culture as well. Society must bring into being numerous pocket subcultures to accommodate the diversity it comprises. There is a need not just for genuine regional cultures but also separate cultures for each profession, as well as a culture for the physically handicapped. Culture is an aid to living the good life, while helping people adapt and merge with their environment. All sorts of pockets of culture are required, not only for the benefit of individuals but also in order that society as a whole may profit.

Modern Design and Japanese Nature

Is Modernism a Product of Northern Culture?

The aesthetic of the lunchbox as cultural leitmotif presupposes a questioning of the nature of the concepts and methodology that went into producing it. The work of giving shape or form to things is broadly termed "design"—but the territory covered is far-reaching indeed. The ceaseless activities of the designer range from popular fashion to graphic design, architecture, and countless other fields. Chief among these, the domain of industrial product design is the territory usually implied by "modern design." It is only natural that the word *design* is profoundly linked in our minds with the aesthetics and teaching of modernism. The modern movement that created and disseminated a "proper shape" for things in the industrial age got its start in England in the middle of the last century and established formal paradigms in Germany during the 1920s—its central ideology being functionalism. It is often said that "form follows function," but, in the final analysis, the key to lasting beauty is the attainment of a simplicity that does away with all extras, including decoration. And the influence of this concept of the greatest possible economy is inestimable.

When addressing various international issues today, confrontational terms such as *east-west* and *north-south* are frequently met. This results from a notion that differences in climate and cultural background give rise to international misunderstandings. But modern design originated in the west and the north, geocultural sectors that had pulled ahead of the rest in terms of industrial development. When speaking of the east-west dichotomy, we envision Japan the easternmost extremity, and yet modern design from the west put down firm roots here. What then about its eventual diffusion from north to south?

61

This geometrical sofa design (1989) uses a functional vocabulary suggesting its esoteric links with traditional Japanese forms. (Photo by T. Nacása & Partners; GK Design Group for Hiroshima City Museum of Contemporary Art)

Even those countries of Southeast Asia and Latin America that occupy southern positions are content to promote design in rhythm with the tempo of their own national goals. It is not wrong to say that *design,* along with technology and management, is still in the cradle stage in those nations—but their aims differ not at all from those of so-called industrialized countries. The newly industrialized economies are today striving to introduce a design culture in the same way we of Japan's postwar design community did in decades past. Whenever I visit one of these countries, every sign, especially conversations I have had with fellow designers, leads me to believe that they, too, will eventually master contemporary design. Just as Japan has, they will turn out well-designed products that hold their own in international competition.

Then I return to the streets with the sun shining brightly among rich greenery. I see a painted scroll of vivid life in which people, animals, and man-made things exist as a single whole. The inhabitants of these countries are indeed poverty-stricken. But there pulses an optimism unique to southern lands, where the necessities of life sprout readily from the earth or tumble from the skies. Then, I cannot help but wonder whether that ascetic functionalism born in the north will ever succeed in putting down roots in this southern environment. In the wafting breezes and brilliant luminosity of the south, I cannot help but feel that modern design is, after all, a product of northern culture. It embodies an inherent monotheistic severity. In these lands of the south, where crowds of *kami* abound in thickets and clumps of grass—sometimes springing out into the road to hold banquets—I feel at the end of the day that modern functional design aimed at economic goals would beat against empty air if it were introduced here. It could only put down roots were it to be adapted and reformed. Just what sort of sea change would modern design require in the process of traveling south?

Japan's Adaptation of Northern and Southern Cultures

More than half a century has passed since modern design entered Japan. And, today, Japan is one of the major producers of advanced industrial goods and packaging. Even before the war, there was a great deal of apprehension among the intelligentsia that modernization would result in decline and disappearance of Japan's traditional culture. But, if viewed from the standpoint of the world of design, there are many issues upon which traditional Japan and contemporary design were in total sympathy. The tendency to simplify and economize; the importance of system as a way of problem solving; and a thoroughgoing spirit of service. In the final analysis, design's present role in the workplace is none other than application of these methods, refined for generations by traditional artisans.

Viewed as design, Japan's traditional culture retains its relevance, above all in its indispensable heritage of "method," which is a veritable treasure trove. Between modern design and Japanese traditional culture there is far greater continuity than disjunction, more harmony than conflict. The nature of the Japanese islands, which lie, so to speak, at the crossroads between north and south, partakes of both regions. In our eager acceptance of modern design's concepts and methods that are so much a product of northern cultural influences, Japan did not simply accept a ready-made package. Rather, we added southern color and fragrance to mold a truly attractive ethos of industrial products. The ability to accomplish this was born from our unique sense of proportion in relation to all things— nurtured in this culture of ours that merges elements from north and south. All we have referred to as a lunchbox aesthetic continues as a creative force, the keynote of day-to-day Japanese culture.

Potential of the Single-Blossom Arrangement

Ultimate Maturity of Civilization

One celebrated episode among the fables and sayings attributed to Sen-no-Rikyu might best be titled "The Single-Blossom Incident." Hideyoshi, powerful ruler of the day, heard of the beauty of the huge morning glories in Rikyu's garden, so he arranged to pay the tea master a visit. That morning, Rikyu went out and cut down the entire multitude of blossoms. He prepared to welcome Hideyoshi by arranging only a single one of these in the decorative alcove of his tea house. Hideyoshi was filled with rage, for owing to his love of extravagance he anticipated a gorgeous profusion. But Rikyu had sensed a limitation in so lively a scene, seeing, instead, infinity in a single blossom. Hideyoshi, who had naively wished to behold a myriad of blossoms, was forced to capitulate to Rikyu's worldview. But recklessly, unable to control his emotions, he ordered the death of the tea master. All flowers condensed in a single blossom, eloquently proclaiming the glory of all flowers.

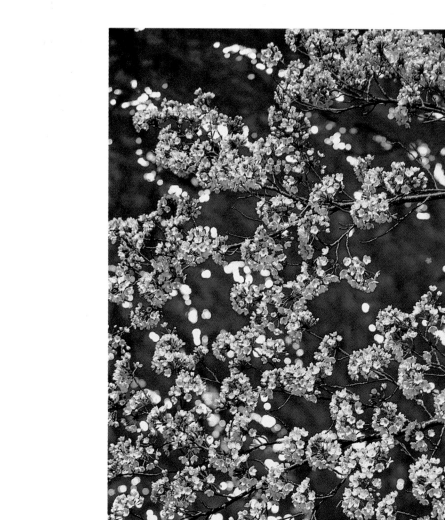

62

Myriad flowers are experienced in a single blossom, demonstrating an infinite complexity in simplicity and the breadth to satisfy limitless desires. (Photo: Fine Photo Agency)

Complex simplicity, simple complexity. Both these concepts are skillfully manifested in the lunchbox. Producing a pack out of diversified elements—just as they are—is one source of the world of the lunchbox. At the same time, there is also a tendency in lunchbox aesthetics to go beyond this ethic of unification.

There is an austerity in the single blossom that the brilliance of the lunchbox is incapable of approaching. It therefore takes a position one step below that of the aesthetic of the single-blossom arrangement, in order to entertain the general public. Meanwhile, the single-blossom arrangement propounds an "infinite" lunchbox, so to speak. All the flowers of the universe are contained and expressed in the single-blossom arrangement. In the one are the countless. The single blossom is not one among many, but rather it is one in which the many are embodied.

What was the emotion that ruled Rikyu's heart as he cut each blossom one by one before Hideyoshi came to visit? He must have luxuriated in the rush of color produced by the morning glories filling his basket to overflowing. But it was a cruel scene, for Rikyu's was the aesthetic of a victor. Moreover, in the beauty of the victor was the martyrdom of countless blossoms. It was out of the master's basket filled to overflowing that the aesthetic of the single blossom was created.

The single-blossom arrangement beautifully expresses the authority of desire, the ultimacy of obsessional deviance. It is a magnificent beauty whose simplicity lies not in the fact that it is single but is, instead, the unification of an infinitude of desire. There are moments when you perceive clearly the three blades of a turning propeller, revolving one by one, for just an instant. Or times when a vigorously spinning top seems to cease in its turning. The more energetic the movement, the clearer the instant of cessation appears. A single blossom is a blossom captured in this manner. It is a complex—yet single—blossom, offering the fleeting image of all blossoms in the universe. And in this adheres the very limitation of its presence. If just one element of the tension in it were slackened, the instant would relapse into confusion. If a single step forward were taken, the moment of perception would disperse as nothingness. Such is the realm of a fully matured high civilization.

Is Japan Still a Lunchbox Culture?

If you take a good look at the situation of Japan nowadays, you encounter confusion on every front owing to the unashamed pursuit of all sorts of desires. It is out of desperation

63

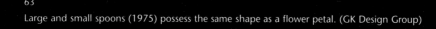

Large and small spoons (1975) possess the same shape as a flower petal. (GK Design Group)

that we have brought this predicament upon ourselves. We have no real talent. Our desires are too shallow. Our greed is too thin.

We no longer have technology for making things or talent for using them. We are at our wit's end in education. Nor have we even the capacity to be bored by it all. This total confusion is misleadingly thrown together as a lunchbox pack and then further pinched into a single-blossom arrangement. We no longer even have hidden intentions—or earnest desires. Of course, a number of items among the multitude of Japanese products have gained from the lunchbox technology of arranging disparate elements together as disparate elements. And there are faint signs of an attempt to replicate a lunchbox technology in many others. But, on the whole, the present situation remains completely outside the lunchbox.

Is it, above all, the difficulty of arranging things well? This agrarian-born people of ours is trying to bend its true nature to become an industrial people with a sophisticated heterogeneous culture. It appears that the waste involved in this process will sooner or later overcome us. Was not the lunchbox itself derived from the need for packed lunches to be taken into the field, as well as for agricultural ceremonies, a complex product of agrarian civilization? Farming is an organic activity that demands service, devotion, and patience as living organisms are helped to survival and fruition. In the past, the technology of daily life was brilliantly perfected. It was a structured technology of aims. There were derivative technologies of brewing and arranging—in short, this was a technology of adapting to the environment. Japan and its agricultural people were adept and skilled.

I am scarcely advocating a return to the rice paddies. I am just suggesting that it might be appropriate to use these familiar technologies and skills in industry as well. Were we to do so, we could ensure a constant flow of beautiful and delicate objects, each of a consummate sensitivity. At this point, I want to recommend a single blossom as symbol of the flower of the skills, arts, and technologies of all agricultural peoples. For this is the concept, and the means, that should be pursued.

I wish to sit for a time just gazing at this single blossom. But even if we are less impetuous than Hideyoshi, such renunciation is too severe. So let us again lay the single blossom carefully to one side, and take the lid off our lunchbox to appreciate the diversity of its contents.

64
A single-blossom vase is designed to bring out the full beauty of one flower. Such vases have been made since ancient times in Japan by craftsmen out of a broad range of materials, including bamboo, ceramics, and diverse metals. The vase shown here is a contemporary object crafted of stainless steel. (GK Design Group)

Conclusion: Spirit of the Lunchbox—Globalization of Japan

The lunchbox is a device that *induces* creativity. First a box is produced and then it is filled with whatever we desire. We have examined its capacity for endless flexibility—creating order in both old things and new. We have likewise seen how the originality of the Japanese, refined since ancient times, still pulsates in the human relations and advanced industrial products of the present day. How can we best preserve and make use of this innate know-how and ingrained sense of beauty in years to come?

The lunchbox way of making things is neither an "-ism," assertion, nor ideology, but rather a technology. It is a matter, so to speak, of engineering. Our lunchbox synthesis is able to cope with the environment, generate order, and enhance the quality of life; it is a technology of structuring, of aims, and of lifestyle. When all these capabilities are brought to bear upon a single product, the result manifests remarkable depth and charm.

Within the confines of this small, densely populated land that is Japan, with its complex natural environment and traditions, this is the sort of brazen, delicate-but-magnanimous technology that has been eked out. We Japanese are said to possess the sharpest artistic predisposition of any people, and this has also born magnificent fruit in applied engineering and technology. For Japan has exerted great efforts toward mastering and using the *technē* of the West.

This same etiquette of production has been unconsciously applied in the creation of the most up-to-date industrial consumer products. This "Japanese way of making things" is embodied in the lunchbox, which is comprehensible to everybody. The lunchbox possesses a "fascination" all can readily understand. It is a functional art—nutritionally sound and wholesome—that goes well beyond mere survival to create fascinating and beautiful things.

It has long been said that the role of industrial design is to realize this very purpose. Yet there is a countertendency asserting that the flood of new products has thrown our daily lives into confusion, that we are now slaves to our new tools. But visit the homes of those who so criticize and compare them with the beauty and order wrought by our best designers. The lack of a sense of beauty on the part of the general public seduces merchants and manufacturers, while driving designers to distraction. The function of design is to assume the stewardship of beauty in the activities of industry. Yet, during the half-century since its inception, Japan's industrial design resources have been demeaned as a cosmetic endeavor affecting mainly the outward appearance of products. But today, design is at last gaining recognition as a key player in the creation and maintenance of the human environment in terms of both beauty and health.

When people come into contact with truly attractive things, they inadvertently reach out toward them. On the one hand, there are no ugly flowers; unfortunately, unseemly industrial products do exist. Since there are those who grab quite randomly at things, such bastard species are rampant.

These products assuage our desires in a straightforward manner, effect a certain unification of diversity, and exhibit a catch-all spirit of service. Such, briefly, are their good points. Meanwhile, the lunchbox and the single-blossom arrangement are economical—but supersede their own asceticism. This resilience has served Japan well up to the present. The lunchbox meal is stylish and delicious. A product of such attraction, such beauty and quality, is desired by anyone and everyone—setting a norm of expectation.

The sensibility involved in the fulfillment of desires must be highly refined. Otherwise, the result is at once something quit *un*refined.

To understand Japan, it is better to depend on things rather than words. For it is things, not words, that tell the story. In this light, the present essay is an inept attempt at putting into words what the lunchbox actually says to us.

Tradition has it that we Japanese lack originality and are adept only at imitating foreign behavior and products. It is certain that we are gifted imitators. But whether or not Japan has its own originality is a different problem altogether. Japan imports its raw materials from abroad. This has been the custom since the prehistoric Jomon age. We begin by replicating an imported object—and later make out of it something quite superior to the original. During the formative Nara and Heian periods (645–1185), the government set up a special workshop for precise imitation of foreign things. Materials were provided to craftsmen of all sorts to copy whatever was brought from China. Even the Meiji government in the last century did the same thing at first, but later discontinued such facilities. We Japanese believe we cannot understand the soul of foreign things, so we attempt to grasp this by making an imitation. Japan was once thought of as a net borrower in terms of culture, but today we have succeeded in refashioning civilization and sending it out again as

65

Design in the spirit of the *makunouchi* lunchbox wills a beautiful appearance incorporating all manner of pleasure, desire, and information within a simple, well-regulated form—such as this monumental sculpture for an Information Plaza in Hiroshima. (Photo by T. Nacása & Partners; GK Design Group)

Japanese. The reason Japanese products sell abroad is the drawing power and flavor of this unique distillation.

Each time I travel overseas, I find the number of Japanese products abroad has increased. Their acceptance is due to an inability to resist the persuasive power of their beauty and quality. I can think of no other way to explain this phenomenon. Superior things have the power to make themselves at home virtually anywhere. Beauty has the great power to deny ugliness. Beauty radiates a warning to whatever gives birth to ugliness. This reception of good things and the persuasion exerted by beauty are forms of civilization. Objects speak for themselves. They act as tiny amplifiers of the spirit of those who made them and of their own innate quality.

There can be no doubt that the sensitivities of people from other countries who have chosen Japanese products are tuned into the frequencies that broadcast the beauty and quality we here in Japan produce. The lunchbox spirit is something that can be understood and absorbed by people the world over. When I see those in other countries buying, enjoying, and using all manner of Japanese goods, I am ever more convinced that everyone possesses tuning bands broad enough to receive this signal of quality.

Civilization promotes our instinct for survival and composure. I earlier defined civilization as a style, culture as scenery. How is scenery engendered in the style of the "heart"? This was once a universal view, and it also typifies Japan's view of the world. Its most ancient method of expression was the mandala in India, while in Japan the same attitude survives in the lunchbox. When we speak of the lunchbox scenery of the Japanese archipelago, we refer more precisely to the image of Japan up to the mid-1920s—the beginning of the Showa period, shortly before the war, when Japan was still an overwhelmingly agricultural nation with a population of between thirty and sixty million people. The lunchbox and its contents represent the aesthetic formulated up to that time.

Happily, we have inherited this aesthetic. It is true that the beauty we sense in the lunchbox is a bit old-fashioned. And that is only natural. But we are now in the process of creating a new representation of the lunchbox structure. This is due to the fact that even quality must be related to scale. The lunchbox technology paradigm will increase in importance; it will necessarily entail assembly at a different dimension from that we know today. But the basic principles and structure of the *traditional* lunchbox are certain to be passed on intact.

I am sufficiently moved by the beauty of the lunchbox to have wished to trace the history of its principles and structure. How satisfying it is that our country has created such force and power that even I, as a designer—whose special field of endeavor is the shape of things—stand in awe. And I believe that the lunchbox comprises a structure of salvation. I have come to realize that its magnificent organizing potential offers salvation for both people and things; indeed, it is a form of salvation just to come into contact with such beauty almost without effort. But its greatest salvation is the realization of a method for living richly with negligible resources. If such a technology can be employed in a systematic manner, it will certainly save the earth.

Among the countries of the world, Japan is far ahead of all others in the depth of its ecological distress. If Japan can discover salvation, the world may also be saved. The limits of growth proclaimed by the Club of Rome were effective in bringing about a consciousness of global limits. Could not Japan's proposal of unbounded containment in a limited space with lunchbox methods afford an apt solution?

The lunchbox mind preaches a providential "way of life" in the face of global crisis. This is a spirit of technology, a *religion* of technology. In advocating beauty and harmony, we must place our trust in a world of things standing symbolically for the world of human beings. There is great need to promote this spirit of technology, this religion of *technē*, today, for technology is a means of realizing desires.

In this book, before anything else, I have considered the lunchbox as a cluster of desires. And to top it off, the lunchbox is beautiful. Here lies my discovery that desire contains the pursuit of harmony and order. Without them, desire cannot attain satisfaction. Beauty in allowing desire its fulfillment is nurtured by harmony and order. This is what human desire is about. If desire be brought straightforwardly to the fore, a rich beauty is born—peace is produced. Unless desire is met thus head on, the result is a falsity in things, a waste—causing strife, which at best is an unprofitable way of proceeding.

The lunchbox has resulted from an energy-saving design. The spirit of the tea ceremony that lies behind it was the *ultimate* energy-saver. This is splendid because the beauty of tea and the lunchbox is not the product of asceticism, but rather of the deep satisfaction of desires. Considered at a global scale, civilization possesses a lunchbox-type character heralded by the advent of the space age—when earth was first viewed from a capsule in outer space.

66

A vermilion-color lacquered *shokado* lunchbox prepared for an autumn day. The small maple branch with bright red leaves adds to the gorgeous colors of the delicacies inside the lunchbox, prepared so the guest can taste the season with both the tongue and the eye. Mostly seafood and vegetables, with cooked rice in a round form and clear soup with a small piece of seafood pudding. (Photo from *Seikatsu Goyomi* 3: *Autumn*, courtesy of Kodansha Ltd.)

67

Paper screens normally hiding a view of the gardens are opened wide to display the autumn scenery. The main "dish" of the day is the brilliant color of autumn leaves. This group of young women is able to enjoy the season with all five senses as they relish the *makunouchi* lunchbox served after a tea ceremony. (Photo from *Seikatsu Goyomi* 3: *Autumn*, courtesy of Kodansha Ltd.)

Today both Japan and the rest of the world must relearn this etiquette of production to achieve resource and energy conservation. Japan has stood from time immemorial for an age of "conservation." And it is thus that we have been able to give birth to rich beauty out of poor things, because in the final analysis we seem to possess the spirit of technology in each and every cell as genetic information. The period of high economic growth had its attractions, but the age to come will be an even more fascinating one for the Japanese people, an age during which we shall be able to make use of our wisdom. The merest glance at the world today makes it clear that we are on the brink of the lunchbox age.

These are ideas focused in an instant as I gazed at the lunchbox. And this book is an explanation of what I saw. I wish to express my gratitude and respect for the lunchbox itself for providing the theme of a useful book. Of course, lunchbox technology is not the *only* kind of technology, nor can it be applied just anywhere. Today as the globe converts into a lunchbox-type environment, the range of application is at last expanding. Inherent ways of creating beauty, order, and salvation underlie every one of the world's regions—embodied in the products of each. This is what *we* must learn from them—while at the same time, I exhort the rest of the world to sample our lunchbox type of Japanese know-how.

Lunchbox technology is a wondrous commodity. Only take a look at this lunchbox meal: Japanese products are all made this way. Yet the lunchbox etiquette of production cannot be patented. A country's "spirit of technology" is hardly a thing whose use should be restricted. Rather, we must exchange it freely, learn from one another, imitate each other, and in general promote a "global regionalism." Japan will continue to contribute to the world in this manner—taking the single-blossom arrangement as its ideal and directing the pleasure of the lunchbox spirit to the rest of the world, as purveyors of "vitamin L."

Appendix   A Brief History of the Lunchbox

Origin

The accepted theory concerning the origin of the *makunouchi* lunchbox maintains that it first appeared as a meal for theatergoers during the Edo period. It has also been claimed that it was first prepared for actors and stagehands in the theater, and that it gradually spread and became popular among audiences as well. In any case, this particular type of meal did indeed establish itself as the major style for theatergoers. There also is a theory insisting that *makunouchi bento* is the generic term that came into use for *all* types of meals served to theatergoers during the Edo period. But in this book, we have used the term only for the style of square box with partitions that contains shaped rice balls and a variety of bite-sized tidbits.

Origin of the Word *Makunouchi*

According to the *Grand Dictionary* published by Shogakkan, the word *makunouchi* is used to denote (1) the outdoor space traditionally designated by cloth curtain partitions for outings and picnics, (2) the area behind the curtain of a theater, in other words, the stage itself or even the actors upon the stage, or (3) the period of time after the stage curtain has been lowered, the intermission or entr'acte, literally the curtain interval. While the strongest claim for the origin of the term *makunouchi* lunchbox is that it was a meal consumed by theatergoers between acts, there is also a theory that it originated as a meal warriors carried—a sort of packed lunch to be consumed in a camp pavilion in time of battle. A final theory relates to sumo wrestling but need not be dealt with here.

The Mankyu *Makunouchi* Lunchbox

A book published in 1853 provides a description of the *makunouchi* lunchbox prepared for theatergoers by restaurants at the end of Edo. After a detailed account of contents and price, the author mentions that such meals were not only served at theaters, but were likewise used as gifts for the sick or on other occasions. According to this text, it was the Mankyu Restaurant in Edo that originated the *makunouchi bento* style; it is even possible that the Mankyu used the term as a sort of trademark for its product.

The Lunchbox in Japan

The general Japanese term for a portable lunchbox is *bento.* It denotes both the meal itself and the container, having been in use since even before the beginning of the Edo period. It refers to lunchboxes for one person or picnic-style provisions for a number of people.

Through the centuries, there have been a variety of different containers created for such specific purposes as mountain work, field work, fishing, traveling, and armed combat. Up until the Muromachi period (1333–1573), when compressed rice wrapped in leaf or seaweed was first served, most portable meals were of dried food. Everyday lunch containers included large leaves, leather pouches, linen sacks, woven straw envelopes, wicker baskets, and round wooden buckets.

The Rice Ball

The wrapped rice ball is Japan's most common portable staple. It originated in the Heian period for distribution to the lower classes at aristocratic banquets, and gradually came into general use under such names as *nigiri-meshi* and *o-musubi.* There are a range of types, including those flavored with salt, those flavored with *miso,* a grilled variety, and those wrapped in seaweed—to name just a few. Originally they were the only food carried as lunches, but when these were served on outings other foods were added, and perhaps this practice is the true ancestor of the *makunouchi* lunchbox.

The Picnic Tradition

Thus we see that the *makunouchi* lunchbox did not begin as a makeshift measure merely to satisfy hunger in a work situation where no other food was available, but rather as a picnic cuisine for outings and celebrations. Typical occasions were related to the annual calendar of Japan's agrarian society. The most popular is still cherry-blossom viewing *(hanami)*. The blossoming of the cherry trees and the opening of the agricultural cycle more or less coincide, creating a perfect opportunity to picnic with the rice-paddy deities under the canopy of cherry blossoms that we Japanese have celebrated since ancient times. It is also said that farmers are able to predict the year's crop by the way the cherry trees bloom. Other popular picnic places are the mountains and the shore. All such occasions are normally accompanied with alcohol, and the food comprises special delicacies sometimes not served in daily meals, making such affairs eagerly looked forward to by persons of all ages.

Cherry-Blossom Viewing

During the Heian period, aristocrats increasingly celebrated the Shinto agricultural cherry-blossom ceremony, gradually shifting its emphasis from the religious to a more purely artistic appreciation of the flowers themselves, as demonstrated in poetry competitions. The high-ranking warrior class also took up the practice, and in 1598, Shogun Hideyoshi gave the biggest and most gorgeous cherry-blossom-viewing party in history at Daigo, in Kyoto. The custom of ceremonial cherry-blossom viewing continued to spread among all levels of the population, until by the early seventeenth century (at the beginning of the Edo period) it had become virtually a national pastime. A number of different types of lunchbox evolved, some of the more sophisticated examples becoming true works of art. These were presented as stacked lacquer boxes fitted with all necessary utensils for eating and drinking outside.

It was during the later half of the eighteenth century in Edo that cherry-blossom viewing took on the form we know today—groups spreading ground cloths under the trees to sing, dance, drink, and eat in a riotous manner beneath the blossoms. This was also when the most famous spots were established for these revels. They included Mukojima in Tokyo, Arashiyama and Daigo in Kyoto, and countless others throughout the land.

Cherry-Blossom-Viewing Lunchboxes

Along with the general popularity of cherry-blossom-viewing parties, picnic outings at other times of the year—and in various places—became widely popular. But the types of lunchboxes that subsequently developed still bore the name "cherry-blossom-viewing lunchbox." Along with sections for food, they contained plates, saucers, cups, pitchers, and chopsticks—all related in design and shaped to fit compactly together. The designs were highly complex and sophisticated, executed in lacquer with inlay of gold, silver, and mother-of-pearl for the upper classes, and with unusual and inventive trick compartments and other surprise effects in those designed for the lower classes.

Most of these cherry-blossom-viewing lunchboxes were large enough to contain servings for a number of people, and they were opened and spread out on a red felt cloth for picnics. Their contents were very similar to those of the *makunouchi* lunchbox today—basically *o-musubi* (rice balls) with a number of side dishes. This lunchbox was not limited to outings and picnics. It was also used to serve groups attending sumo matches and the theater.

Theatergoing Customs

A number of special customs originated among the enthusiastic theatergoing wealthy merchants and townsmen of Edo during the first two decades of the nineteenth century (in the Bunka and Bunsei eras). In those days, attendance at the popular Kabuki theater was an all-day affair; intervals between acts were the scene of elegant socializing among actors and members of the audience. Wealthy patrons competed to provide gorgeous lunchboxes to their favorite performers, who, with their entourage, deigned to consume these in the box seats with their patrons. The custom became a ritual of status for theatergoers. Outfitting themselves in new clothes for the occasion, they took pains to purchase specially made lunchboxes filled with exquisite delicacies. Thus the customs surrounding theatergoing took people away from the sumptuary restrictions of their everyday lives into an entirely different world of fantasy.

The Theater Tea House Lunchbox

Theatergoing in the Edo period permitted and encouraged eating and drinking during the performance. Tea houses near the theater grew up in Kyoto, Osaka, and Edo. The larger of these had their own kitchens, while the smaller ones depended upon independent cooks in kitchens some ways away to deliver prepared foods. Attendants from the tea houses would greet the guests upon arrival at the theater and provide them with extra mats to sit on and utensils for smoking. At lunchtime, these waiters would appear again with *makunouchi* lunchbox meals, and later in the afternoon they might deliver snacks of sushi and sweets. The food containers were matched sets of stacked lacquerware boxes.

The *Kaiseki Makunouchi* Lunchbox

The earliest type of lunchbox was the matched set of stacked boxes typified by the cherry-blossom-viewing lunchbox, as well as the individual portable lunchbox made of unfinished wood, which is still common today under the simple name of *bento* or *bento-bako*. The more formal style we know today as the *makunouchi* lunchbox developed as part of the tea ceremony, particularly for outdoor tea gatherings, as a simplified version of the formal banquet style known as *kaiseki ryori*. The contents as well as the style and shape of the lunchbox could be altered to fit the requirements of the particular gathering.

The literal meaning of the word *kaiseki* is "stone in the stomachband," referring to the time-honored custom of placing a warm stone against the stomach to appease hunger when food was unavailable. Thus *kaiseki ryori* implies a meal sufficient to warm the stomach and satisfy the hunger temporarily. The concept is said to originate in the vegetarian meals of Zen monasteries where the austere norm has for long been a single bowl of soup and two vegetable dishes. As stated in the text, the great perfecter of the tea ceremony Sen-no-Rikyu is credited with adapting the *kaiseki* banquet style to the tea ceremony during the 1570s. The present form and style in terms of both content and box shape were reached during the eighteenth century. The main difference between lunchboxes for theatergoers and for picnics and the tea ceremony lunchbox style is the gorgeousness and plentifulness of the former as opposed to the austere elegance of the latter.

The *kaiseki* lunchbox contents remained in the realm of the Zen monastery vegetarian style, but animal protein and fish dishes were added to make it more generally appetizing. In modern times, with more inclusive menus, it spread from the tea ceremony to more general occasions and also to Japanese-style restaurants. Still, it stood apart from the strictly portable lunchbox types in being served by the host rather than brought separately by each individual guest. Since World War II, it has spread as a popular, convenient way to serve a simple but delicious meal to almost any number of people who have foregathered for any social or business purpose.

Various *Kaiseki* Lunchbox Types

The most popular lunchbox used for the *kaiseki* lunchbox meal is the rectangular *makunouchi* lunchbox that is the theme of this book. But there are other shapes as well. These include a moon-shaped one of which Sen-no-rikyu is said to have been particularly fond, an oblong one, a fan-shaped one, and a hemispherical one. This last consists of several shallow layers and is said to have been favored by the great warrior Shingen Takeda (1521–1573), whose name it often bears. Finally, there is the *shokado* lunchbox—perfectly square with four equal square partitions—described in the text and discussed below.

The *Shokado* Lunchbox

This is the lunchbox that enjoys the greatest popularity in traditional Japanese restaurants (as opposed to shops that specialize in mere fast-food, or take-out-style, meals). Creation of the *shokado* lunchbox is attributed to an early seventeenth-century Zen priest named Shojo Shokado (1584–1639), famous as a tea master, writer, and painter. The story has it that he was inspired by a container for farm seeds, and that he began by using this as a smoking box, with one partition to hold tobacco, the second for flint, the third as tinderbox, and the fourth as ashtray. There is a rival tale claiming that he converted the seed box into a medicine chest. In any case, lunchboxes with partitions have been in vogue since the Heian period. The earliest examples were made of unfinished Japanese cypress wood. An illustration is known from a painting dated 1715 that is exactly the same shape as the *shokado* lunchbox.

During the late 1920s, the Kitcho Restaurant in the Koraibashi district of Osaka hit upon the idea of serving meals in square containers with four equal partitions; this, it would seem, is what came to be called the *shokado* lunchbox. After World War II it came into general use as a picnic box, mainly owing to an increase in chances to eat out of doors.

At the Kitcho Restaurant, the contents of the *shokado* lunchbox are set in a manner very similar to that of other *kaiseki*-style *makunouchi* lunchboxes: with pieces of raw fish in the upper right-hand section, vegetables in the upper left-hand section, boiled foods in the lower left-hand section, and shaped rice in the lower right-hand section. Other restaurants do not adhere so strictly to any fixed arrangement—the only common feature being that rice is relegated to one or other of the lower sections.

The Station Lunchbox

Today most people relate the *makunouchi* lunchbox more to train journeys than to traditional-style restaurants. The station lunchbox is a cross between the picnic lunchbox and the practical strip-craft lunchbox for those involved in farm work, mountain work, or military maneuvers. The first station lunchbox appeared with the opening of the new railway line that linked Tokyo's Ueno Station with Utsunomiya in 1885. It was quite a simple affair containing two wrapped rice balls flavored with pickled plum *(umeboshi)* and covered with grilled sesame seeds, with a couple of slices of radish pickle *(takuan)*, the whole wrapped in a piece of bamboo bark, and sold for five sen, or a few pennies. Moreover, it was sold exclusively for coming up from the country at Utsunomiya Station. The first station lunchbox in recognizably *makunouchi* style that contained a variety of food items and was packed in an unfinished wooden box went on sale at Himeji Station to celebrate the opening of the Sanyo Line in 1888. Its popularity derived mainly from the fact that the different delicacies it contained were not readily available to the general household in those days, giving it a gala atmosphere somewhat akin to the earlier and more elaborate theater and picnic lunchboxes. It was meant to enhance the joy of train travel, just becoming popular in Japan at that time.

During the last decade of the nineteenth century, a three-tiered lunchbox was most prevalent, but by the end of World War I it had given way to the two-tiered variety. Then in 1921, the Kobe Railway Company came out with a rectangular lunchbox with a single partition, as opposed to the former square type with four partitions, giving birth to the most common shape of station lunchbox today. Subsequently, higher-priced lunchboxes went back to the two-tiered style that had prevailed up to the time of World War II. It was not until 1965 that the average station lunchbox returned to the single-tier arrangement. Station lunch-boxes today are generally divided into "ordinary" and "special" types, the main difference being quality of contents.

The *Makunouchi* Lunchbox Today

Sit-down lunchbox restaurants appeared first around the turn of the century, later developed into more general eateries during the 1920s, and have diversified and increased in numbers ever since. As a result, lunchboxes lost much of their relevance, with dining out taking their place. The individual variety has almost lost its purpose for workers, school children, and even picnics. A streamlined, thin-gauge aluminum lunchbox appeared around the turn of the century that became virtually emblematic of the ubiquitous white-collar worker, giving these persons the nickname of "the lunch-at-the-hip tribe." But today this utilitarian lunchbox is definitely a thing of the past. And the custom of local authorities providing lunch for students has further reduced opportunities for the younger generation to partake of lunchbox meals.

The trend toward a lessening of contact with the lunchbox in daily life gave rise, ironically, to a renewed popularity of high-class products in both the *shokado* and the *kaiseki* lunchbox traditions as light meals for entertaining guests.

On the other hand, the ordinary prepared meal today mass-produced for sale in department stores and supermarkets has taken on a variety of aspects. Made of Styrofoam or clear plastic, it contains a dizzying array of foods. There is a recent trend toward customizing these fast-food lunchboxes in accordance with specific orders while the customer waits. This trend has also affected the *makunouchi* lunchbox. The quality of the contents of these mass-produced lunchboxes is appallingly low, making them an entirely different breed from their gorgeous ancestors. In many cases, the rice is no longer even shaped or wrapped but simply crammed inside the assigned partition. And there are many, especially among station lunchboxes, for which the rice shapes have been molded by machinery, in imitation of the wooden molds long used for shaping rice in traditional lunchboxes.

There are also firms today that mass-produce something close to the traditional *makunouchi* lunchbox and deliver it in bulk for company lunches or large gatherings, such as conventions and sports rallies, packing them in disposable plastic single-layer or tiered boxes.

Nevertheless, the better-quality lunchboxes produced today still boast a variety and quality that recall the traditional *makunouchi* lunchbox spirit.

Rice Consumption and the Future of the *Makunouchi* Lunchbox

The history of the *makunouchi* lunchbox reveals a great many changes in all aspects, including container, arrangement, and contents—yet shaped rice has always maintained its place in one form or another, and the general rule has been to fill the lunchbox with dry foods, or moist solid preparations that retain form.

Beginning around the 1920s, a type of lunchbox meal known as a "Eurasian lunchbox" began to appear with a combination of Japanese and Western foods. But since rice may be eaten with almost any food, this did not make for any drastic change in tradition. Finally, since there is no evidence of rice losing its position as the main staple of our Japanese diet, it does look as if the *makunouchi* lunchbox will prevail as the principal type of lunchbox commodity in Japan well into the next century.